HITLER'S LAST DAY

HITLER'S LAST DAY

THE FINAL HOURS OF THE FÜHRER

RICHARD DARGIE

Picture credits
All photographs by Getty Images

This edition published in 2022 by Arcturus Publishing Limited
26/27 Bickels Yard, 151–153 Bermondsey Street,
London SE1 3HA

Copyright © Arcturus Holdings Limited

All rights reserved. No part of this publication may be reproduced, stored in a retrieval system, or transmitted, in any form or by any means, electronic, mechanical, photocopying, recording or otherwise, without prior written permission in accordance with the provisions of the Copyright Act 1956 (as amended). Any person or persons who do any unauthorised act in relation to this publication may be liable to criminal prosecution and civil claims for damages.

AD006424UK

Printed in the UK

MIX
Paper from responsible sources
FSC® C018072

Contents

Prologue
Final Dawn, 30 April 1945 7

Chapter 1
Last Will and Testament, 29 April, 12.10 a.m. 13

Chapter 2
The Wedding, 29 April, 12.30 a.m........................37

Chapter 3
Disintegration, 29 April, 11 a.m. 61

Chapter 4
Terror and Revenge, 29 April, 2 p.m. 85

Chapter 5
Fading Hopes, 30 April, 6 a.m. 107

Chapter 6
Death of a Warmonger, 30 April, 3.25 p.m. 129

Chapter 7
Aftermath, 1 May, 6 p.m. 151

Epilogue
Misinformation and Myths..................................175

Further Reading:
Eyewitness Accounts 187

Mini-glossary 188

Index 189

Prologue
Final Dawn, 30 April 1945

At around 7.30 a.m. on the last morning of his life, Hitler started to climb the concrete steps that led up from the Führerbunker to the bomb-shattered garden of the Reich Chancellery. He was well aware that these were likely to be his last few hours on earth. His new bride Eva had been up in the garden just a few minutes before and had probably encouraged him to go and get a last breath of fresh air, away from the foul mixture of diesel and stale urine that permeated the rooms and corridors of their underground home.

He took his time, making very slow progress up the concrete staircase, as the tremors in his left leg were more regular and more pronounced than before. When he had almost reached the heavy security door that led outside, he stopped short of the exit and stood there for some minutes. Perhaps he was deterred by the sound of heavy Russian shelling above or maybe it was the thought that in a few hours his remains would lie just a little beyond that bomb-blast door.

Looking back at the past
In recent weeks, Hitler had fallen into reminiscing about happier days in Berlin. He had greatly enjoyed entertaining

The last-known picture of Adolf Hitler after he left the bunker in Berlin to award medals to members of the Hitler Youth.

friends for afternoon tea in the Chancellery garden in what now seemed to him the far-off golden years of the 1930s. Here he had chatted with the lovely Baroness von Laffert and with the bright and sparky Leni Riefenstahl. He had also entertained clever and ambitious young Nazi officials and ambassadors from friendly and hostile nations, all desperate to listen to his every word and judge whether his plans for military and territorial expansion were realistic or just hot air. Now he knew that the garden he loved was just a heavily cratered landscape that reminded him of the wasted Great War battlefields of France and Belgium. His final companions there would be Eva, who had decided to die with him, and the 15 or so patients who had expired in the operating theatre of the makeshift underground hospital nearby and been buried in the Chancellery courtyard.

He had recently spent time remembering and describing his first visit to Berlin on leave from the Western Front, staying with the family of an army comrade and discovering the treasures in Berlin's many museums and galleries. He loved his boyhood home of Linz on the Danube and he had been entranced by Vienna and Munich, the cities of his later youth and early manhood. But it was the vast boulevards and the dark and impressive architectural beasts of Prussian Berlin that had swept away the adult Hitler. This was a city where emperors had ruled and where armies had marched to and fro. It was the place where he had spent most of his time during his great years as one of the most powerful and hated dictators of the 20th century.

He believed he had added to Berlin's rich heritage by giving it new adornments in the National Socialist style: the New Reich Chancellery and the Olympic Stadium. But he had also dreamed of transforming Berlin into a new, larger city, Germania, that would be worthy of being the capital of a Reich that would last for a thousand years and stretch from the Atlantic to the Urals. Now, in a few hours he would be dead. The powerful, ruthless and corrupt political movement that he had created would collapse and the dream of empire that had powered his every thought and action would evaporate.

Did he feel any remorse?

In these last moments of his life, did Hitler reflect upon the years of organized terror, total warfare and horrific extermination that he had unleashed upon Europe and the world? Did he feel any guilt for the millions of deaths that were the direct result of his political ambitions? His political testament, written the day before he committed suicide, reveals that he died unrepentant, convinced of the rightness of his cause and his actions. If his testament was an opportunity to express regret for the horrors of his regime and his responsibility for the deaths of millions, often in the most squalid and inhumane circumstances imaginable, that opportunity was not taken. It was devoid of any sense of remorse or apology. The blame lay entirely with others. He had always been right, he thought: it was his enemies who had been wrong, mistaken, deluded. Above all, he continued to blame abstract foes such as the Jews, who had fuelled his earliest rants in the beer halls of Munich.

Did he feel any regret at leading Germany into an unwinnable war and an abyss of despair and degradation? His explosion of anger and frustration eight days before his death suggests that he did not feel at all responsible for the catastrophic failure of his leadership and the collapse of the government of the Third Reich that he had overseen. It was, in fact, the German people themselves who must take the blame, he firmly believed. The German people had not been worthy of him. They had failed to rise up to the historical challenge of his mission to create a master race that would dominate the world. In his eyes, he had fulfilled his duty as Führer but others, especially the treacherous army generals, had betrayed him by their failure to carry out his orders to the full. Now, it seemed, even senior figures in the National Socialist movement had also undermined him.

Sociable and sociopathic

It is unlikely that this most complex of historical characters felt any regret or remorse for the immense human misery that his policies of racial war and extermination had brought about. The old man standing still on the bunker steps did not judge himself by the moral standards of ordinary men and women. Instead, he believed that his only moral peers were the great commanders of the past, such as Alexander, Hannibal, Caesar and Napoleon, although the war had shown that he himself had little of their tactical and strategic genius.

It was this belief that gave him the ability to be both sociable and sociopathic. Though he was undoubtedly friendly, courteous and charming to his friends, acquaintances and subordinates, he could turn to his desk and approve plans that sent millions of innocent people to horrible deaths in the extermination camps, at the hands of Nazi machine-gunners in the forests of central and eastern Europe or through 'annihilation by labour', the Nazis' term for the appalling treatment of the underfed slaves within their empire. None of this caused him to lose a moment's sleep throughout his 12-year reign. It was, in fact, the very reason for his political being.

His duty, he believed, was to 'cleanse' the continent and rebuild a stronger, 'racially purer' Europe. If his historic mission was incomplete at his death, he had certainly done everything in his power to make it possible. He might have lost the military war against the Allied Powers but time would sort that out, he declared. Germany would survive the disaster of 1945 and rebuild, though 'some of its feathers would be ruffled' in the process. In his view, his actions would not be judged by some temporary Russian or American tribunal but in the eternal court of history. He did not believe he would be found wanting.

Now he accepted that nothing survived of the old Berlin that he once bestrode as a colossus. It was but a desert of rubble and dust. He stood before the closed bunker door for a moment more, then slowly descended the steps, turning his back upon the world forever.

Chapter 1
Last Will and Testament, 29 April, 12.10 a.m.

At about ten minutes after midnight on 29 April 1945, Hitler asked his secretary, Gertraud 'Traudl' Junge, to sit with him: he had decided to kill himself and was ready to dictate his Last Will and Political Testament. Traudl was the youngest of his four private secretaries and although she was only 25 years old she had worked closely with Hitler for three years: in the Reich Chancellery in Berlin, at Wolfsschanze or Wolf's Lair, his military command post in East Prussia, and at his Bavarian summer home, the Berghof, in Obersalzberg. Now she found herself fated to share Hitler's last days in the Führerbunker. She was an excellent secretary and she was also devoted to Hitler, who had always treated her in a kind, fatherly manner. After the war she confessed to a deep sense of guilt at having been fond of a man who was responsible for so much mass murder and horror.

Hitler quietly informed her that he was going to dictate two documents. The first was a private will with instructions for the disposal of his personal assets after his death. The second document, however, by far the more important of the two as far as Hitler was concerned, was his political testament, which would deal with his historic legacy and would contain his last commands regarding the government of what remained of the Third Reich. While he carefully dictated the testament he referred to his written notes and Traudl rightly supposed that this was the text she had seen Hitler and Joseph Goebbels discussing privately over the previous few days.

All hope gone

With all of the false lingering hopes finally extinguished, Hitler now accepted that the war was irredeemably lost. He had entered the Berlin bunker on 16 January 1945, just after the events of the Battle of the Bulge had fully exposed Germany's incapacity to halt the Allied offensive. He had stayed on in Berlin to keep the faith with those remaining German troops holding out against a vastly superior opponent and to maintain civilian morale. Or perhaps his acceptance of defeat was brought about by deep despair and his declining physical condition. But by refusing to desert Berlin he also had one eye on history: he would not be remembered as a coward fleeing from his last crumbling fortress.

By April all hope of avoiding total defeat and unconditional surrender had gone. There would be no miracle. No relief column breaking through the Red Army lines that encircled Berlin. No new wonder weapon that would clear the Allied planes from the skies above Germany. And to make defeat more bitter, some of his closest, longest Party allies had betrayed him. There was bad news too from Italy: his ally Mussolini had been captured and his own troops there were now surrendering. The limited German command

The ruins of the German Chancellery, with the entrance to the bunker and the turret from which the SS men kept watch, Berlin 1945.

structure that survived was focussed around dwindling enclaves near the Baltic coast, where Admiral Dönitz and Himmler still commanded remnants of the Wehrmacht and the Waffen SS.

It was only a matter of time before Russian troops stormed the Reich Chancellery, only a few hundred metres away. Most of the bunker personnel had left, many of them ushered to safety in Bavaria at his own command on some of the last flights out of Berlin. Others had quietly disappeared to take their chances among the burning rubble of the city.

The communications room in the bunker was now virtually silent: few messages for the Führer were coming in from the field. Local commanders were making their own decisions to preserve what remained of their units and the lives of their men. In any case, German signals capability was almost defunct. Radio contact was intermittent: frantic messages from the Führerbunker to the troops still fighting in the streets above were now scribbled on paper and carried by volunteer runners from the Hitler Youth. Hitler realized that he no longer mattered. If the Nazi Reich was to continue in some form, Hitler now accepted that he had no part in its future.

Hitler draws into himself

In the last week or so of his life, since his explosion of impotent rage on 22 April, Hitler had drawn into himself, taking increasingly little interest in the events unfolding above in the burning streets of Berlin, saying little even when picking at his daily lunch with his secretaries. Much of his time was now spent with his German shepherd Blondi and her pups. When he spoke at lunch, he said little about the war but preferred to ramble on about the principles of caring for dogs and training them well. Now, with the realization that there was very little time left, he was concentrating on tidying up his personal affairs and on the important task of leaving a justification of his ideas and deeds for posterity. And he had just enough time to settle a few private scores.

Private will

Hitler's private will was brief. Other than books and a few pieces of art that had sentimental value, Hitler had never much bothered about owning material possessions. He was inspired by ideas and history, rather than things and the fleeting pleasures of the world. While some Nazi leaders such as Göring and Himmler sacked museums and art galleries across Europe to amass their treasure, Hitler's art collection had been acquired for a specific purpose. As a boy he had spent his formative years in the city of Linz in Upper Austria and had always looked upon it as his home town. He had long dreamed of transforming Linz into the cultural capital of the Greater Germany that would, he thought, dominate the future of European civilization.

In 1941, when the entire continent seemed to be in his grasp, he commissioned the architect Hermann Giesler to begin the task of planning and building this new Führerstadt. However, other more pressing wartime tasks had consumed Giesler's time and energy and it was only in February 1945 that he finally completed his model of the Linz of the future and delivered it to the New Reich Chancellery.

Architect Hermann Giesler shows Hitler his plans for Linz.

There, while his real capital city collapsed around him, a distracted and entranced Hitler spent hours examining and discussing every aspect of Giesler's grand vision of a city that would never be built. Hitler had always planned to retire to Linz once his political mission was complete, but now he accepted that he was going to die in Berlin. All he could do was bequeath his pictures to his home town on the Danube.

Bormann's rise to power

In his will, Hitler appointed Martin Bormann to act as the sole executor of his estate. Since 1943, Bormann had held the title of Personal Secretary to the Führer and as a result he exercised immense power and influence over all ranks of the Nazi Party, including the Führer himself. He had joined the Party relatively late, in 1927, but by then he had already built a reputation in extreme right-wing circles as a sound, reliable fellow. His credentials included his vigorous membership of the paramilitary Freikorps in the early 1920s; his deeply held hatred of the Jews; his friendship with Rudolf Höss, later Kommandant at Auschwitz; and his involvement in at least one brutal political murder.

Martin Bormann was a squat, lumbering man who knew that he lacked the swaggering demeanour required of a leading National Socialist. He was, however, a dedicated, tireless and cunning bureaucrat who was willing to take on and master all of the dull, difficult legal and administrative duties that others avoided. By 1933 he was on the edge of the Nazi Party's ruling elite, serving as personal secretary to the Deputy Führer, Rudolf Hess, until his dramatic flight to Scotland in 1941.

Transforming the Berghof

Bormann was by then also serving Hitler in a direct capacity. In 1935 he was given the job of supervising the transformation of the Führer's small chalet in the Alps, Haus Wachenfeld, into a fully equipped governmental hub where Hitler could relax with friends and members of the Nazi elite, or host and impress foreign dignitaries. At the Berghof, as the chalet was now called, Bormann already acted as Hitler's personal secretary, a post that gave him continual access to the Führer and the opportunity to control the access of others. In time Hitler became heavily dependent on Bormann, who was now the spider at the heart of the Nazi web, controlling information, rumours, decisions, squabbles and appointments. His influence over Hitler made him many enemies but also gave him immense power, which he exercised quietly, effectively and ruthlessly.

Takes over from Hess

In 1941, Bormann assumed Rudolf Hess's role as Head of the Party Chancellery, giving him control over most German domestic affairs. Moreover, he soon exercised increasing influence over the civilian government of the conquered territories in the East. It was Bormann who signed the decrees that established the extermination camps which would facilitate 'the final solution to the Jewish Problem' and which gave Adolf Eichmann the authority to start organizing the detailed destruction of European Jewry.

Bormann was much less well-known to the German people, and to foreign observers, than the high-profile trio of Himmler, Göring and Goebbels, who had very publicly accompanied Hitler throughout the Nazi Party's rise to power in the 1930s. Yet by 1942 Bormann held such a concentration of state and Party power in his hands that he could quite rightly regard himself as a very likely contender to succeed Hitler as Führer.

Bequests to family members

Hitler trusted Martin Bormann completely. In his will, he gave Bormann full power to decide how much of his estate should be left to his family, only stipulating that each member should receive enough for 'the maintenance of a modest simple life'. Hitler had loved his mother Klara

Martin Bormann lends an attentive ear to his master Adolf Hitler in conversation with von Ribbentrop. Admiral Dönitz is isolated on the far left and the tall man (back to us) in the foreground is Hitler's valet Heinz Linge. Behind them, a trim Mussolini chats with a bulky Hermann Göring at the Wolf's Lair, 1944.

very deeply and her early death in 1907 from breast cancer devastated him. However, his feelings for most of his other relatives were cool and his contact with them was only ever sporadic and limited.

Adolf was never particularly close to his younger sister Paula, who saw very little of him until his emergence as a major national figure in the early 1930s. He supported her financially to some extent, but seldom met her in the flesh. Nevertheless, in the last weeks of the war he did order Bormann to make sure that he got her out of Berlin and off to the safety of his mountain retreat at Berchtesgaden in the Bavarian Alps. Hitler saw more of his half-sister Angela, who acted as his housekeeper at the Berghof in Obersalzberg from 1928 to 1936. The Führer was, however, not particularly upset when she left his household that year in protest at the growing influence of his mistress, Eva Braun.

Hitler's nephews

Hitler also still had two living nephews in 1945. Angela's son Leo was in Soviet hands, captured two years earlier at Stalingrad while serving as a flight engineer in the Luftwaffe. Although Hitler was fond of Leo, at the height of the battle and with the German forces surrounded, he pointedly refused to fly him out of the closing Soviet trap, fearing accusations of favouritism. He did later consider exchanging Leo for Stalin's son Yakov, who had been taken prisoner by the Wehrmacht in 1941 in the first month of the 'Barbarossa' campaign against Russia, but the response from the Kremlin to this suggestion was not encouraging. Leo languished in Soviet captivity until 1955.

His other living nephew, the part-German, part-Irish William Patrick Hitler, had grown up in Liverpool and only visited Germany briefly in 1933 and 1938, hoping to see what his famous uncle could do to help him progress in life. Hitler is said to have called William 'loathsome' and probably never accepted him as a real member of his family.

He had been much fonder of his third nephew, Heinz, an enthusiastic National Socialist who had studied at an elite military academy before joining the Wehrmacht as a signals officer in 1941. Posted to the Eastern Front, he disappeared in January 1942 after making his way to a forward position to retrieve radio equipment. It isn't clear if Hitler ever knew whether his favourite nephew had been killed or captured. In the event, Heinz ended up in the old Tsarist prison of Butyrka in central Moscow. In Soviet times, it often housed 'distinguished' political and military prisoners. After several days of interrogation and torture, he died in Butyrka in late February 1942, aged 21.

After making provision for his surviving relatives, Hitler specifically indicated that Eva's mother, Franziska 'Fanny' Braun, should receive a distribution from his estate.

Co-workers remembered

Also remembered were the 'faithful co-workers' who had formed the intimate team around him, both in Berlin and at the Berghof. Only one member of this group, Frau Winter, the housekeeper of his apartment in Munich, was actually named in the document, but Bormann knew exactly who Hitler meant when he expressed his thanks to those 'who have for many years aided me by their work'.

Hitler disliked change in his immediate household staff and preferred to be surrounded by familiar faces who understood how he liked to live and work. Many of these co-workers had served under him throughout the years of Nazi rule and they had come to form almost a substitute family. All of them were devoted to him and never escaped from the magic spell that he cast upon those around him, even in his final, weakened days.

His longest-serving secretary, Johanna Wolf, had been with him since 1929 and was typical of the deeply loyal staff around him. It was only with the very greatest difficulty that Hitler could persuade, or rather order, her to leave Berlin for Bavaria on 22 April. His chief aide Julius Schaub was a veteran of the failed Munich Putsch in 1923, a fellow inmate of Landsberg Prison and a founder member (No. 7) of the SS. Friend as much as servant, Schaub served as Hitler's aide from 1925 until the collapse of the Third Reich. He was only absent from Hitler's side at the very end because he was already in Bavaria, busy carrying out the Führer's order to destroy all of his personal files in Munich and Obersalzberg.

His personal pilot, Hans Baur, had flown Hitler to Party meetings and rallies around Germany since the early 1930s. His deputy pilot, Georg Betz, also remained in the *Vorbunker* (forward bunker) above Hitler's rooms throughout the last days, waiting and hoping for the order that never came to transport the Führer to safety. Erich Kempka was an original member of the SS Führer Escort Command and graduated to the role of principal chauffeur when Hitler's old comrade, friend and driver Julius Schreck died suddenly of meningitis in 1936.

These were typical of the men and women who formed Hitler's court at the very centre of the Nazi universe. Hitler understood and appreciated their contribution to his regime and remembered them in his last hours. After rewarding these old retainers from his estate, anything of value that was left was to be given to the Nazi Party. If that no longer existed, Hitler ruefully continued, the remnants should be given to the German state. If that had also ceased to exist, the defeated warlord concluded that 'no further decision of mine is necessary'.

Political testament

In his political testament, Hitler reflected on his life of service to Germany, which had begun in 1914 when, although a subject of the Austrian Crown, he volunteered to fight for Kaiser Wilhelm's Reich. The document ran to almost 1,500 words and summarized key ideas from speeches he had made throughout his political career and especially in the years after war broke out again in 1939.

The war was not his fault, he claimed; he had always argued for peace in Europe, wishing to avoid a repeat of the 1914–18 catastrophe. Had he not met with the British ambassador in late summer 1939 and proposed a peaceful solution to the German–Polish crisis? Had he not argued for plans to control and limit armaments?

It was the leading circles in English politics, by which he meant the 'gangster' Churchill (Churchill also described Hitler in this way) and his cronies, who had rejected his offers of peace, he asserted. It was the current leaders of Britain who had wanted war, in part because war was always good for business and also because they were in thrall to international Jewry. In Hitler's view, the Jew, the international conspirator in the world of finance, was the real criminal behind 'this murderous struggle', which had resulted in the deaths of millions of the children of Europe's Aryan people. In time, he declared, the guilt of the Jews, of statesmen of Jewish descent and of those who worked for Jewish interests, would be recognized by all.

Why Hitler stayed in Berlin

Hitler then explained his decision to remain in the capital of the Reich until the very end. Although in his anger he had expressed his disappointment with the German people and had declared that they were not worthy of him, he would share his fate with them all the same. He would not take the cowardly way out by abdicating or surrendering, but confirmed that he would 'of my own free will, choose death at the moment when I believe the position of Führer and Chancellor can no longer be held'. Ever the frustrated artist and actor, he also knew that a dramatic death in Berlin was a more fitting end to his career than a hanging in an Allied prison.

He continued his testament by expressing his thanks for the courage and sacrifice of the soldiers at the Front and the workers, farmers and women at home, and as ever mentioned with pride the deeds and achievements of the 'Youth who bear my name'.

He acknowledged the special bravery of the men and women such as Bormann and Goebbels who had stayed by his side uniting 'their lives with mine until the very last'. These he now begged and ordered to leave so that they could continue to fight 'the further battle of the Nation'. Instead of perishing with him in Berlin, they should continue their work of building a renewed National Socialist state in which citizens were obliged to serve the common interest. This in Hitler's desperately unrealistic view was the work of the coming centuries.

New leaders named

His next task was to name the principal office-holders in the regime that he thought would succeed him, further evidence of his delusional state of mind at this stage.

Admiral Dönitz would serve as Reich President; Goebbels as Chancellor; Martin Bormann would continue to be responsible for NSDAP affairs as Party Minister; and the former Reichskommissar of the Netherlands, Arthur Seyss-Inquart, was named as Foreign Minister. A further 14 cabinet ministers were also named and Hitler appointed Ferdinand Schörner as commander-in-chief of the Wehrmacht. It was a reward for Schörner's total dedication to National Socialism and his legendary ruthlessness both against the enemy and against any of his own men thought to be defeatist and shirking their duty.

The Luftwaffe was now to be commanded by Robert Ritter von Greim, a 1914–18 war ace and a veteran of the Munich Putsch, as well as being Hitler's old friend. The only problem was that the Luftwaffe was an air force that no longer existed.

A few days earlier, on 26 April, Greim and his co-pilot, the Hitler loyalist Hanna Reitsch, had been ordered to fly to Berlin to meet the Führer. Making their way through heavy anti-aircraft flak, which badly wounded Greim in the foot, they managed to put their small Storch aircraft down in the Tiergarten park, within shooting distance of the Red Army. In gratitude for this final pointless act of loyalty, Hitler promoted Greim to Generalfeldmarschall, another hollow title by this stage in the war.

Having named the men who would command Germany after him, Hitler ordered these new leaders to continue the war against the Allies by every means possible. He also charged them to observe the 1935 Nuremberg Race Laws and to mercilessly oppose 'the universal poisoner of all peoples, international Jewry'. These instructions confirm just how out of touch with military and political reality Hitler had become in his months below in the bunker, and how little he realized just how quickly and completely all things National Socialist would be swept away once he departed the scene.

A fallen star

There were two significant absentees from this proposed new administration: Reichsmarschall Hermann Göring and Reichsführer Heinrich Himmler. Both of these men had helped to create the National Socialist state but both had been toppled from their positions of authority in the last few days of Nazi power, at least in the paper plans of the bunkered dictator if not in reality on the ground.

Göring was arguably the best-known Nazi after Adolf Hitler. A fighter ace in the First World War, a badly wounded veteran of the Munich Putsch and an early commander of the fledgling *Sturmabteilung* or SA, the bully boys of the Nazi movement, Göring was one of Hitler's favoured Old Fighters. The personal bond between the Führer and Göring was formed in 1922: Göring joined the Party that year immediately after meeting and hearing Hitler for the first time. In the early months of the Third Reich in April 1933, Göring played a key role in establishing the fundamental means by which the Nazis controlled and repressed the German public – the Gestapo.

With his background in aviation, in 1935 Göring found himself responsible for quietly building up an effective German military air force, the Luftwaffe, in contravention of the Treaty of Versailles rules limiting German rearmament. In the late 1930s, he masterminded the four-year industrial and military plan to make Germany ready for a European war by 1940. After the rapid blitzkrieg victories against Poland and France, in which the Luftwaffe played a leading role, Göring was by far the most popular Party leader after the Führer. Hitler recognized this by nominating Göring as his successor in September 1939 and by bestowing on him the title of Reichsmarschall, the highest German military rank, the following year. Göring's status as Hitler's preferred heir was officially confirmed by decree in late June 1941.

Broken promises

After that, Göring's star waned badly and RAF Bomber Command soon made a mockery of his foolish boast that not a single bomb would fall on the Ruhr, Germany's industrial heartland. His own bombers had also failed to subdue the RAF in 1940, making a future invasion of southern England unlikely, and soon it was clear that the Luftwaffe lacked enough planes and pilots to win a war that was now being fought on multiple fronts. The Luftwaffe's dwindling reserves were then squandered on the wasteful Ardennes campaign in late 1944, handing almost total control of German skies to the Allies.

Göring's promised wonder weapons, the new jet aircraft like the Messerchmitt 262 and the Arado bomber, were never produced in sufficient numbers to make a significant impact. Over a thousand jet fighters had been promised but fewer than 60 were operational by the time D-Day arrived. And Hitler eventually grew tired of Göring's over-optimistic situation reports. Increasingly bypassed by Hitler and the High Command, Göring retreated to Carinhall, his hunting lodge in Brandenburg, to spend more time examining his art treasures and preparing their shipment to his home in Bavaria. His last visit to the Führerbunker on 20 April, Hitler's birthday, was noticeably short. The exhausted Führer was curt with his old colleague and quickly dismissed a man whom he felt had let him down badly.

Charged with treason

Retiring to Obersalzberg, Göring spent the next few days considering Hitler's diminished personal condition and his isolation in the centre of an encircled city. The 1941 decree that named Göring as the Führer's deputy was clear. In the event that Hitler could no longer act freely as Germany's leader, full powers within the Third Reich would fall upon Göring's shoulders. And had Hitler himself not said several days before that only he, Göring, could negotiate a reasonable peace with the Allies? Besides, if he did not replace Hitler as Germany's leader, his bitter rival Bormann certainly would.

Accordingly, on 23 April he sent a cautiously worded telegram to the Führerbunker. It suggested that as Hitler

Göring and Hitler after the assassination attempt of July 1944. This photo was banned by Hitler because he disliked the anxiety and fatigue betrayed in their postures and on their faces.

now seemed unable to act freely, he would assume control if no reply came from Berlin by 2200 hours.

Unfortunately for Göring's plans, the telegram reached Bormann first, not Hitler. Armed with other evidence of Göring's preparations for leadership, Bormann had no difficulty in persuading his exhausted boss that Göring's telegram was treason. After a burst of fury, Hitler stripped Göring of his titles and powers and in his testament he confirmed Göring's disgrace, nullifying the 1941 decree and expelling him from the Nazi Party. Bormann instantly ordered the senior SS officer at the Berghof to arrest Göring and execute him if and when Berlin fell to the Russians. Only the loyalty of a small Luftwaffe detachment in Bavaria saved the former Reichsmarschall from murder at the hands of the SS. Seeing no way out, he quickly made his way westwards and into the safe custody of the US Army.

Himmler's betrayal

The other disgraced Party leader was Heinrich Himmler. An intelligent, well-educated man with a college education in agronomy, Himmler was also an early member of the Nazi Party and the SS. A hard-working, talented administrator, he was quickly spotted by Hitler and appointed to key positions in the Nazi Party in his native Bavaria. In 1929, Himmler became the commander of the SS and, in 1934, after the Nazi takeover, he was put in charge of the Gestapo. Two years later, in 1936, he was made chief of all German police organizations.

Himmler was an avid pupil and friend of the racist ideologue Richard Walter Darré, a Blood and Soil eugenicist, who believed that the principles of natural selection should be applied to the populations living in the eastern European territories that Nazi Germany would capture: the inferior Slavic stock would be rooted out and replaced by hardier Germanic colonists.

First concentration camp

Less than three months after the NSDAP seized power, Himmler established the first concentration camp at Dachau. He quickly founded the Death's Head SS, a special unit designed to carry out the elimination of groups that were 'no longer required' in Germany, such as Jews, Gypsies, Communists and inconvenient intellectuals. After the lightning conquest of Poland in September 1939, Himmler's special operations task forces, or *Einsatzgruppen*, efficiently wiped out the Polish leadership class, shooting or hanging over 65,000 prisoners in the first three months of the war. The *Einsatzgruppen* carried out mass executions in the forests and shooting pits of places such as Piaśnica, honing the skills in mass murder that would be used again and again throughout eastern Europe and Russia in the coming years.

Racial policies

Like Hitler, Himmler saw the war in the East as 'a question of existence, a racial struggle of merciless severity in which millions of Slavs and Jews will be annihilated by military operations and by failures in the food supply'. Himmler was the patient, thoughtful and meticulous administrator who planned the destruction of the *Untermenschen* who had no place in the New Europe. More than any other Nazi leader, apart perhaps from his stern acolyte Reinhard Heydrich, Himmler sought to implement Hitler's dream of a 'racially pure', anti-Bolshevik Greater Germany, stretching from the Rhineland to the Urals. And although the two men were never personally close, Himmler was the one Nazi leader who always discussed his activities with Hitler and received his instructions from him in the strictest privacy. In the last days of the Reich, Hitler was outraged but not overly surprised by Göring's treachery in attempting to replace him as Führer. But he was deeply shaken and dismayed when he learned that he had also been betrayed by the man he called 'the loyal Heinrich'.

Surrender offer

Like Göring, Himmler visited the Führerbunker on 20 April to attend the brief ceremony marking Hitler's 56th birthday, where both men expressed their deep, unwavering loyalty to their leader. Himmler knew, as Göring did, that Hitler was finished, so he left Berlin and never returned. He clung to the hope that, with Hitler dead, Britain and America would come to their senses and unite with what was left of Germany to fight their real enemy, Soviet Russia.

Well aware that the war was lost, Himmler had already put out feelers to figures in neutral Sweden in a vain attempt to open communications with the Western Allies. He met with the Swedish Count Bernadotte, who represented the International Red Cross, on 23 and 24 April in the old Baltic port of Lübeck. As a sweetener, he had already given the nod to the transfer to Sweden of some 13,000 Scandinavian citizens languishing in German camps and prisons.

On 28 April, however, Radio Stockholm claimed that Himmler, claiming to be the effective German head of state, had offered to surrender his forces unconditionally to the

British and Americans. The claim was later confirmed by Reuters and the BBC. When it reached the bunker, the impact of this 'news' on Hitler was poisonous. The commander of the SS, the most dedicated National Socialist organization, who wore the motto 'My honour is called Loyalty', had stabbed him in the back. The exhausted Hitler summoned up what energy he had left for a final explosion of rage. Several hours later, in his dictated testament, he expelled Himmler from the Party and from all of his state offices for 'secretly negotiating with the enemy without my knowledge and against my will, and for illegally attempting to take control of the State'.

Arrest of Fegelein

Hitler could not inflict any real punishment on the traitor Himmler, who was on the northern coast of Germany near Kiel, where he was planning to meet Dönitz so he could offer to serve under his command. Under arrest in the bunker, however, was a high-ranking SS officer who was one of Himmler's 'creatures'. Hermann Fegelein had certainly seen some action in the East against the Red Army and also much action against Russian civilians, masterminding the liquidation of over 23,000 civilians and Russian prisoners in a single 'military operation' in 1941. This zeal in the cause of National Socialism helped his rise to the position of one of Himmler's senior adjutants. The marriage that he engineered to Eva Braun's sister Gretl in June 1944 also helped.

However, on 25 April, with the Red Army closing in on the government quarter of central Berlin, Fegelein disappeared. He had booked out the last service vehicle in the bunker, claiming that he had been sent out on reconnaissance duties. Instead, he was found by the Reich Security Service on 27 April in his apartment. He was drunk, wearing civilian clothes and in the company of a semi-naked young woman who was not Eva Braun's sister.

A packed suitcase contained his passport, clothes, jewellery and cash in sterling and US dollars: clear evidence of a planned desertion. But his fate was truly sealed by the locked attaché case found in his rooms. This seems to have contained evidence of Himmler's attempts to communicate with the West, which had been entrusted to Fegelein for transfer to a Scandinavian go-between.

Eva briefly pleaded with Hitler to show some mercy for her sister's husband but didn't press the matter when she realized that Fegelein was a lost cause. He was shot among the bomb craters in the Reich Chancellery garden a little before midnight on 28 April. His corpse was still warm when, a few metres below, Hitler informed Traudl Junge of his intention to marry Fegelein's sister-in-law that very night.

Hitler's marriage announcement

In fact, Hitler's very first thought in his private will was for Eva Braun, a friend and member of his social circle in Munich since 1929, and certainly his mistress since 1932. She had lived a privileged but secret and much restricted life with Hitler throughout the years of the Third Reich and as German defeat came ever closer she made it clear to friends in Obersalzberg that she would remain faithful to Hitler until the very end. On 7 March 1945, she ignored his order to stay in the relative safety of Bavaria and took the train for Berlin to be with him and, most probably, to die with him.

Now, Hitler explained to Traudl, he had decided to mark the loyalty of 'that girl who, after many years of faithful friendship and of her own free will, entered the practically besieged city in order to share her destiny with me'. He wanted to compensate her for 'what we both lost through my work in the service of my people'. Eva would die with him as Frau Hitler and not as the Führer's mere concubine.

Chapter 2
The Wedding, 29 April, 12.30 a.m.

On the evening of 28 April, Hitler informed Goebbels of his decision to marry his mistress and ordered him to find an official capable of performing the wedding. A qualified registrar was quickly located. Walter Wagner was a 37-year-old lawyer in Goebbels' propaganda ministry but had been drafted into the Reich's civilian militia, the *Volkssturm* or People's Storm. His unit was conveniently stationed near the Reich Chancellery and was awaiting the next Red Army onslaught. Bundled into an armoured car by SS guards and driven through the rubble, Wagner was taken down to the heart of the Führerbunker and informed of his task.

After a delay while the awestruck Wagner was first driven away to his office to get the correct documentation and then returned by the SS to the waiting bride and groom, the wedding began at around half past midnight. It was held in the conference room, where the usual clutter of maps and despatches on the table had been swept away.

The bride wore a simple black dress, a traditional colour for brides in Germany before the war, and the groom wore a grey military jacket, a style that he adopted at the outbreak

On top of the world: Hitler with Eva Braun in happier days at the Berchtesgaden retreat in the Bavarian Alps. This photograph was found among Braun's personal possessions.

of war in 1939. He felt that it suited his role as military commander of the nation better than the partisan brownshirt look of earlier days.

In his NSDAP uniform and *Volkssturm* armband, the registrar was excited to be in the presence of the Führer but managed to steady himself enough to speak in a calm, low voice. As required by Nazi law, bride and groom affirmed that they were of Aryan origin and free of all polluting hereditary diseases that would bar them from marriage. They confirmed their willingness to take each other as man and wife and then exchanged gold rings supplied by the Gestapo, probably from its treasury of loot stolen from its victims across Europe.

Wagner offered the marriage certificate and a thick blue pen to the Führer, who quickly scribbled three zigzags and a cross to designate his first name, more artistic logo than signature.

The surname followed in a neater, more legible hand. Eva signed in a clear, simple italic style but had to scratch out the B that came to her automatically and write her new surname instead. Goebbels and Bormann signed as witnesses.

Throughout the brief ritual, exploding Russian shells and the shuddering vibrations from a direct hit on the bunker's thick concrete roof added to the nervous tension that is usual at nuptials.

Wedding reception

Despite the circumstances, champagne, wine, tea and a spread of sandwiches were available at the reception; the wine cellars and food stores of the Reich Chancellery had not yet been ransacked by the advancing *Frontviki*, or front-line troops of the Red Army. In addition to the Goebbels family, there were six wedding guests: Bormann, generals Burgdorf and Hewel, Artur Axmann, chief of the Hitler Youth, Gerda Christian, one of Hitler's four private secretaries, and the Führer's long-serving adjutant for Luftwaffe matters, Nicolaus von Below.

Given that the bunker might have been overrun by the Soviets at almost any moment, the atmosphere in the group was relaxed and they sat and chatted for over an hour.

For these few brief moments, Hitler seemed able to shrug off the catastrophic events unfolding above. A very moderate drinker of alcohol, he indulged himself with a small glass of Hungarian wine sweetened with sugar. His new bride was particularly adept at lightening the mood by telling tales of what had been for them happier times.

First meeting with Eva

Hitler first met Eva in 1929 when she was 17 and working as an assistant in his friend Heinrich Hoffmann's photographic shop in Munich.

She was standing high on a shop ladder while reaching for files on the top shelf and feeling self-conscious. Understandably perhaps, because she had recently shortened the skirt she was wearing, possibly by a few centimetres too many, and was aware that she hadn't done a very good job.

At that moment she noticed the man standing below her, wearing a beige belted Burberry raincoat and sporting an unfashionable *Rotzbremse* or snotbrush moustache. He was gazing intently at her legs.

HITLER'S SEXUALITY

Homosexuality rumours

Throughout Hitler's life there was much speculation about his sexuality as well as many rumours, most of them originating from his rivals and enemies and seldom backed up by real evidence. Nevertheless, some threads in Hitler's life were woven into a suspicion that his sexual taste was for men rather than women. It was rumoured, long after the event, that he had participated in homosexual acts in the men's hostel where he stayed in Vienna in the years before the First World War. In his time on the Western Front, he was certainly known as a quiet, reserved young man who chose to read and sketch while his comrades visited the beer tents and field brothels in the rear: clearly this was evidence of a lack of physical interest in women.

Hermann Rauschning, an early National Socialist, later claimed that Hitler had been found guilty under Paragraph 175 of the Imperial German Legal Code, which penalized 'unnatural fornication between persons of the male sex and between humans and beasts'. Others pointed to the prominence of men such as Ernst Röhm and Rudolf Hess within Hitler's early leadership circle: Ernst Röhm was the flamboyant homosexual leader of the SA and Rudolf Hess the starry-eyed sycophant who stood by his beloved Führer throughout his imprisonment in Landsberg Castle.

And there was Hitler's close friendship with Emil Maurice, his chauffeur and the victor of countless bloody street battles throughout the 1920s against the enemies of the NSDAP. Their friendship was certainly a deep and lasting one, which Hitler honoured in 1935. When the SS discovered that Maurice's ancestry was tainted with Jewish blood, he bestowed his personal protection and the privilege of Honorary Aryan upon his old comrade.

Fetishistic desires

Others sought to discredit and diminish Hitler by suggesting that he was prey to bizarre fetishistic desires. It was whispered that he had forced his half-niece Angela 'Geli' Raubal to indulge his stranger requests, leading to her depression and suicide in 1931. In 1943, a team of CIA psychoanalysts, including some of America's most prominent psychologists and psychiatrists, were instructed to profile Hitler in order to better understand him. They came to the conclusion that he was a coprophile.

And apparently Hitler was also a masochist. After a private dinner one evening in his quarters in the Reich Chancellery, it was said that he prostrated himself at the feet of his beautiful guest, the film actress Renate Müller. He then wept and begged her to kick and humiliate him, the story goes. Confused and fearful of the consequences of offending such a powerful man, Müller fled but was later found dead on the pavement below her third-floor hotel room. These tales and similar bits of street gossip were used to vilify Hitler. They spread widely and were often believed: because his political views and brutal actions were so abhorrent to so many it stood to reason, said his critics, that his private life must also be abnormally vile.

In fact, very little of the mud thrown at Hitler's private life was ever made to stick, no matter how often it was repeated by sensationalist journalists in later decades. Long after his death, one of his friends from his hostelling days in Vienna, August Kubizek, dismissed any idea that the young Hitler was gay. Kubizek remembered only too well the lovesick Hitler's intense infatuation with a pretty young female in Linz. He followed her about town and lusted after her from afar, but due to his personal insecurity and lack of sexual experience, he never even spoke to her.

In fact, the German Army records kept on his conduct throughout the period from 1914 to 1920 indicated that his personal behaviour had been consistently very good and he had incurred no penalties for infringements of the military code. There was certainly no evidence of a court-martial for the bestial and pederastic practices alleged by Rauschning. But his accuser had his reasons for trying to blacken Hitler's reputation. In the 1930s, Rauschning had fallen out of favour with Hitler, left the Nazi Party under a cloud and then expressed support for centrist political parties that advocated German–Polish cooperation. As a result, he had fled to the USA rather than end up in a Nazi 're-education camp'.

Detested homosexuals

Hitler's avoidance of the dubious delights of the field brothel in the First World War probably stemmed from his political and scientific reading rather than from any psychotic dislike of women. Hitler was already reading and absorbing current popular theories about racial hygiene and purity: soldiers who went with French whores, he concluded, ran the risk of contracting syphilis and other venereal diseases. They weakened themselves as soldiers and as potential fathers and therefore enfeebled the army and the German nation.

The homosexual Röhm was certainly a key member of the NSDAP power structure in the 1920s when Hitler needed him. He was, however, one of the very first to be liquidated in the murderous Night of the Long Knives in 1934, when Hitler swiftly eliminated all those influential Party members who posed a threat to him.

Hitler claimed that he detested homosexuals on ideological grounds, because they deviated from the National Socialist vision of a pure Aryan German people consisting of burgeoning families under the guidance of a strong father and a fertile mother. His views underpinned the Nazi legislation that resulted in the wearing of the pink triangle in concentration camps and the torture and deaths of many thousands of homosexuals between 1933 and 1945.

The Geli Raubal enigma

Hitler was certainly very fond of his niece Geli but there is no evidence of a sexual relationship with her, or that his grief at her death was anything other than mourning for a beloved relative who had died in sudden and distressing circumstances. The psychoanalysts working for the CIA were very largely influenced by the testimony of Otto Strasser, a prominent Nazi in the 1920s, who had quarrelled with Hitler and then fled to the USA. His brother Gregor, a leading figure on the extreme right wing of that period, had also quarrelled with Hitler but remained in Germany.

Although Hitler at first allowed Gregor to return to his civilian life as a chemist, he was murdered when the long knives came out in the summer of 1934, suffering a particularly slow death when the SS shot him and left him in jail to die of his untreated wounds. As a result, Otto hated Hitler intensely and doubtless took great pleasure in relaying the old street gossip from his Berlin days that Hitler had either ordered Geli to urinate and defecate on him or that he had wanted to besoil her. The CIA shrinks naively mistook Strasser's bizarre accusations for evidence, rather than a mixture of vengeful bile and the desire to please his new American masters.

As for Hitler's abasement before and beneath Ms Müller, no evidence was found to confirm this episode but after the war her sister Gabriele did scotch the myth that she either threw herself from her hotel balcony or was thrown by Gestapo officers. Renate, she said, had died in hospital from complications following an operation to her leg.

Hitler's friendships with women

Lacking serious evidence to the contrary, most professional academic historians have concluded that Hitler was most probably conventionally heterosexual, but that for various personal and political reasons he kept this part of his life very private and quite limited in scope. The gauche young Hitler of the First World War certainly admired women from afar but seemed to lack confidence around them. However, the mature Hitler who emerged as a dynamic, and for many a charismatic, figure on Germany's political stage in the 1920s found it much easier to make friendships with women.

Maria 'Mitzi' Reiter

Maria 'Mitzi' Reiter was certainly smitten by the future Führer when she met him in 1926. Like Eva Braun, Maria was Bavarian and much younger than Adolf. She was also similar to Eva in that she was pretty and pleasant, a shop worker and no intellectual. It seems that Hitler wanted her as a lover and as a secret mistress but not as a wife, though he offered to marry her once he had fulfilled his national mission.

But unlike Eva the role of mistress was not enough for Mitzi, who dropped Hitler just as his political career was taking him ever further away from Bavaria. After the war, Maria claimed that Hitler asked her three times to be his mistress, the last time being in 1934 when he had become Führer. She also claimed that she spent a night of successful intimacy with Hitler in Berlin in 1931. This cannot be proved, but Hitler's sister Paula certainly confirmed that her brother was deeply enamoured of Maria and was saddened when they drifted apart. He sent 100 red roses to her in sympathy in 1940 when the Obersalzberg hotelkeeper she had ultimately married was killed in action at Dunkirk, but the pair never met again.

The passionate supporter

As Hitler transformed himself from a provincial beer hall tub-thumper into a powerful national politician, the women that featured in his public life were increasingly of a very different stamp: they were talented and well educated and they mixed in the highest levels of German society. A number of these influential and prominent women admired him deeply and remained close to him throughout the Nazi era. They offered Hitler specific gifts and opportunities that matched his interest in music, culture and politics and some may have offered physical pleasures as well.

Helene Bechstein, who had married into the world-famous piano manufacturing family, was a very close friend and an important patron. Without her affection and support, he might never have risen above the other rabble-rousers that infested German gutter politics in the early 1920s. Helene introduced Hitler to her society friends, all wives of Germany's leading men, but only did so once she had improved his table etiquette and sharpened up his public demeanour. She remained loyal to him after the disastrous Munich Putsch that seemed to have ended his career in 1923 and she visited him frequently in Landsberg Prison.

The gift of a red Mercedes-Benz from the Bechsteins raised Hitler's confidence at a low point in his career and also gave him an important practical and symbolic tool for projecting himself as a national and not merely a regional political leader. Helene and her husband picked up the travel expenses for Hitler's early speaking tours around Germany and helped the NSDAP to develop and circulate its *Völkischer Beobachter*, or People's Observer, newspaper. As a sign of her enduring loyalty Helene finally joined the Nazi Party in 1944, at a point when many Germans were beginning to try and disassociate themselves from it.

The cultured admirer

If Helene offered access to the top industrial and financial echelons of German society, Winifred Wagner ushered Hitler upwards to the glittering peak of Germanic culture. An Anglo-Welsh orphan, Winifred was fostered out to distant German relatives in 1915. At the age of 17, Winifred married Siegfried, son of the great Richard Wagner. Siegfried was himself a successful composer but he was almost 30 years older than Winifred and bisexual. The marriage had been engineered by the wider Wagner family. They hoped that the young and sparky Winifred would distract Siegfried from his male paramours and encourage him to provide heirs to continue the Wagner line – thereby maintaining the family's control over their cultural and financial assets in Bayreuth.

Winifred surpassed all expectations, serving up four children by 1920, at which point Siegfried rather faded out of domestic Wagnerian life and spent much of his time and energy elsewhere. This left Winifred the space to devote herself to the politics of the Wagner family, to the administration of the annual Bayreuth Festival and to the

Adolf Hitler with Winifred Wagner at Haus Wahnfried on the opening day of the Bayreuth Festival, 1937. Also in civilian clothes are her sons Wolfgang and Wieland.

serious but impressive political adventurer that she probably first met at Helene Bechstein's salon.

Winifred was in Munich during Hitler's failed putsch and witnessed key episodes of the fiasco. She sent parcels to Hitler in prison, including stationery for Hitler's plans to write a political masterpiece. Nazi lore had it that her gift was used by Rudolf Hess as he scrambled to scribble down Hitler's hurried dictation of *Mein Kampf*. As well as an intense passion for Wagner and all things Wagnerian, Hitler and Winifred also shared similar political values: Winifred had read and admired the anti-Semitic works of the English writer Houston Stewart Chamberlain and her love of Wagner's Romantic music had seduced her towards Aryan *völkisch* political attitudes. While Winifred gave Adolf access to the family and the home of his ultimate hero, Adolf gave Winifred the possibility of embedding Bayreuth at the heart of a future *völkisch* Germany.

The couple grew closer after Siegfried's death in 1930. A Party member since 1926, Winifred often appeared alongside Hitler on his election campaigns across Germany throughout the late 1920s and early 1930s. They often ended up staying in the same country inns and hostelries, which fed the gossip in Munich's restaurants and salons that Winifred had found both a soulmate and a physical replacement for her late husband. Numerous observers spotted them walking hand in hand in the grounds of the Bayreuth Festival Theatre or at Haus Wahnfried, the Wagner mansion. When in Bavaria, Hitler would often arrive late at night at Wahnfried and leave early the next morning.

Several members of the Wagner family certainly believed that at one point in the early 1930s Hitler was considering marrying Winifred. However, after Hitler became Chancellor in 1933, affairs of state directed his energies elsewhere and enforced a greater distance between the couple, although they remained close friends. By the time Hitler visited the epic 1936 Bayreuth Festival, he had spent the intervening years moulding Nazi Germany in his image. By then, Winifred had turned Bayreuth into a powerful shrine to Nazi symbolism and ideology.

They continued to exchange valuable gifts, however. Winifred woke one morning to find that a Daimler Benz limousine had materialized outside the Wahnfried portal and, on Hitler's 50th birthday, she gave him the original scores of Wagner's *Das Rheingold* and *Die Walküre* and the draft manuscript of his favourite Wagner opera, *Rienzi*. He was overcome and deeply moved.

The beautiful princess

Baroness Sigrid von Laffert was almost born to be the perfect escort for the Führer. She came from an aristocratic family that had espoused the Nazi cause and she was charming, intelligent and able to sustain an informed conversation about Hitler's key interests of art, architecture and music. Not only that, she was a committed National Socialist, having enrolled in the League of German Maidens, the female counterpart of the Hitler Youth, as a young teenager and before membership became compulsory. She joined the Nazi Party itself in 1938, once the membership was reopened.

And she was an Aryan beauty – tall, slim, elegant and blonde. The Italian Foreign Minister, Galeazzo Ciano, who was an expert in these matters, noted her 'clear eyes, her perfect features and her magnificent body', while the

Italian ambassador to Germany, Dino Alfieri, was similarly impressed by 'her provocative bust, long legs and the sweetest little mouth in the world'.

Sigrid wore very little make-up, something which pleased Hitler, and often wore her long, plaited hair in the traditional and politically correct Germanic crown. From 1934 onwards, 'Sigi' frequently took a prominent place in Hitler's entourage at public events such as Party rallies in Berlin and Nuremberg. She sat with him in his box at the Berlin Opera House, attended state dinners in the Reich Chancellery and was certainly keen to be a more permanent figure in the Führer's life. Hitler's adjutant, Fritz Wiedemann, heard Hitler asking her why she had not yet married and remembered her coquettish reply: 'You know perfectly well why not.' Sigi was waiting to be asked by her Führer.

Sigi and Winifred, and the quixotic photographer Leni Riefenstahl, in whom Hitler took a passing personal interest until she turned down his suggestion to make a film about the Nazi martyr Horst Wessel, could take their places in the Nazi pantheon, but they were not what Hitler was looking for in a permanent companion. They were highly cultured, well-educated women who were interested in politics and already enjoyed their own independent place in society. As women who were in the public eye and enjoyed being there, they would only distract Hitler from his work. And they might divert the attention of the German people away from their leader.

Possible partners

Hitler had never forgotten the advice of his friend and mentor Dietrich Eckart, the writer, dramatist and anti-

Semitic politician who had vigorously promoted Hitler in the early days. Eckart looked for the Coming Man who would rescue Germany from the humiliations of the Versailles Treaty and the machinations of the Jews. That man would have to be completely focussed on his mission of national salvation, even if that meant all kinds of personal sacrifices. And said Eckart, shrewdly: 'He must be a bachelor, then we'll get the women.'

Hitler knew that he could never share the public stage with one of these beautiful, intelligent celebrities. That might diminish his appeal for the millions of ordinary German women who felt or dreamed that they had their own special relationship with 'their' Führer. It may also have been that Hitler did not feel equal to the task of competing with these talented and educated creatures on a daily basis. He had always felt constrained by his relatively humble origins and his lack of formal education. Although his private libraries in Munich, the Berghof and Berlin provide evidence of his voracious reading, he remained the classic insecure autodidact who often felt inferior to the qualified men around him, such as his architects Speer and Giesler.

Hitler needed a partner who could provide the necessary domestic comforts but who would be happy to take a secondary place in his life. Someone like Mitzi Reiter, who was uninterested in the world of politics and government, who shared his lower-middle-class background and who would understand what was required of a companion, homemaker and mistress. But Mitzi had turned him down. Perhaps the young assistant in Hoffmann's shop was the woman he was looking for.

HITLER AND EVA BRAUN

Early days

Eva Braun was Bavarian by birth and upbringing. Her grades at school and business college had been unexceptional, but she was pretty and athletic and had developed into a pleasant and confident young woman when she met Hitler in 1929. She was flattered by his invitations to smart cafés and restaurants around Munich and she quickly became part of the wider circle that hung around him in places like Café Heck and Osteria Bavaria. Gradually, Eva moved ever closer towards the centre of Hitler's private life, becoming his mistress in 1932 after the death of Geli – and after Bormann had confirmed the Aryan purity of her family bloodline.

In these early years Eva twice attempted suicide, episodes that seem to have been designed to extract more attention and affection from her often-absent lover. The second attempt in 1935 was possibly inspired by Hitler's growing friendship with Baroness Sigi, a relationship that, unlike hers, could be made a little more public in the Nazi media. By then Hitler's life was based in Berlin and his visits to Munich were infrequent, but she continued to receive flowers, gifts and telephone calls when he could drag himself away from the task of reconstructing Germany as a rigidly totalitarian state.

Whenever the Führer was in town, Eva packed her small suitcase with what she nicknamed her 'screwing kit' and made her way to meet him at his apartment on Prinzregentenstrasse, a short walk from the eastern bank of the Isar river in Munich. On the occasions when she travelled with Hitler's court to public events around the Reich, Eva always remained Fraulein Braun and assumed the role of a secretary or a photographer. In time, she and her sister Gretl moved into an apartment that Hitler rented for her in Widenmayerstrasse, close to his own flat, using the Hoffmann photographic agency as cover for the rent and expenses.

In early 1936, he presented her with the gift of her own detached house in the upmarket district of Bogenhausen. It cost him 300,000 Reichsmarks, some of the vast royalties he had collected from the sales of *Mein Kampf*. At the height of the Sudetenland crisis in 1938, when Hitler was wary that a major European war might break out, he made his first private will. Eva was his main beneficiary. He gifted her a monthly pension of 1,000 Reichsmarks, a far more generous bequest than to any of his relatives.

Moving into the Berghof

In 1936, Hitler paid Eva the compliment of bringing her into the heart of his emotional world by settling her in the Berghof, the mountain home that was being transformed from a modest holiday chalet into a vast and impressive Führer complex. After a brief and victorious skirmish with Hitler's half-sister Angela, who soon quit her post as housekeeper at the Berghof, Eva was confirmed as its undisputed chatelaine. Here she ruled over her coterie of friends: her sister Gretl, Frau Hoffmann, Margarete Speer, wife of Hitler's friend and architect, and Anni Rehborn, champion swimmer and wife of one of Hitler's doctors, Karl Brandt.

Eva lived in a gilded cage but this had its own magnificent compensations: a life of luxury in the beautiful Alpine world and trips to Italy with her friends. She enjoyed taking regular exercise in the lakes and mountains of the Obersalzberg, developing her skills with a cine camera and shopping anonymously in Salzburg after the Nazi takeover of Austria in early 1938. At the Berghof, the staff understood her unique status in the Führer's life, learned to call her Madam and for the most part also began to like the woman who was mistress of the house when 'the Chief' himself was away from home. The calming effect that she had on the Führer and the atmosphere of happy, relaxed domesticity – the *Gemütlichkeit* or comfortableness – that pervaded the Berghof was quickly noticed by most of the wives of the Nazi elite, helping Eva gain their respect.

The secret mistress

It was only when foreign dignitaries such as the Duke of Windsor or Neville Chamberlain were present that Eva retreated into the shadow of the Unterberg mountain above the Hof. When Hitler required a female escort in his public duties, the role was usually performed by one of the leading Nazi wives, often Magda Goebbels but sometimes Emmy Göring, until she offended Eva and was excluded from the Berghof by Hitler. Eva's name never appeared in the 140-strong list in the Berghof telephone directory and on the rare occasions when she was in Berlin she used her own special suite of rooms in the Reich Chancellery but had to come and go by the staff entrance and eat alone in the apartment. Berghof regulars understood that Eva's existence was a state secret and would be a dangerous one to divulge, so the German public knew nothing about Eva Braun until the very end of the war.

Their sexual relationship

In all other respects, the relationship between Adolf and Eva seems to have been normal. Their adjacent rooms at the Berghof had an interconnecting door and staff grew accustomed to finding Eva in her nightgown, sitting with the Führer late at night in his study. She often took him a snack and they shared a small glass of schnapps. His long-time valet Heinz Linge recorded one embarrassing occasion when he entered their private room and found them in 'ardent embrace'. Long after the war, Linge observed: 'Hitler and Eva Braun had been especially active on occasion. I do not know which of the two was the more active but Eva, in the modern terminology, could be very sexy and so I suppose was Hitler.'

After the war, the housekeeper at the Berghof, Gretel Mittlstrasser, disclosed that she liaised with the house doctor to refresh the supply of contraceptives when required. Eva herself joked about the physical side of their relationship when showing some of her friends a photograph of Neville Chamberlain sitting on a sofa in Hitler's Munich flat in 1938. The British Prime Minister had been blissfully unaware, she laughed, of the 'goings-on that sofa has seen'.

The wartime propaganda that Hitler was impotent or suffered from some kind of genital deformity seems to have been just that: propaganda. During the war, Soviet propagandists were particularly keen to diminish their arch-enemy by spreading rumours of varying credibility: Hitler was impotent; his genitals were deformed from birth; his penis had been bitten in half by a goat when he was a youth. However, medical records from when he was a child, when he was in military service in the Great War and after he was wounded in the bomb blast on 20 July 1944 provide no evidence that he was deformed or physically unusual in any way.

Dr Erwin Giesing, the army doctor who examined Hitler thoroughly after the assassination attempt at Wolfsschanze, found no signs of physical abnormality, nor any visible signs of him having contracted a venereal disease. The rumours to that effect probably originated in Hitler's frequent use of syphilitic imagery in his speeches, which often warned of the ways in which contact with Jews and other *Untermenschen* might pollute the Aryan race. The belief that Hitler had only one testicle probably originated in the lyrics of a version of the popular British Army marching song written by Toby O'Brien, a sharp-witted publicist at the British Council. The song was also wrong about Goebbels, who successfully fathered six children with his wife Magda.

Mutual fondness

Life at Obersalzberg was not always idyllic. Hitler could be curt with Eva, especially if she irritated him by bursting into his study while he was deeply engrossed in thinking or reading about some difficult political or military dilemma. He sometimes called her *Tschapperl* or 'bumpkin', an ambiguous term that could be rendered affectionately but also in a way that pointedly reminded her of her humble, parochial origins. She often remarked to friends that she had grown tired of listening to his ranting and hearing the same old stories about the early days of the Party in Munich and that she also despaired of his poor dress sense, which made him look like 'the eternal sentry'. On the other hand, the staff at the Berghof were in no doubt that the couple were fond of each other. Whenever Hitler discussed his future life after politics, he painted an idyllic picture of Eva and himself living quietly in Linz.

They were not openly affectionate and maintained the facade of being merely friends in front of servants and occasional visitors such as Hitler's barber August Wollenhaupt, who travelled from Berlin to Bavaria as and when required. But even he could see that Hitler enjoyed Eva's company and was more relaxed and happy when she was around. Wollenhaupt also noted that Hitler seemed to have grown fonder of Eva the longer they were together. During the war, when he was often far from Munich for long spells, he made a point of phoning her every second day and he detailed Bormann to send on his letters to her accompanied by flowers.

Joining Hitler in Berlin

Eva understood that she was never to intrude on the political side of Hitler's life, but during the war she did so twice on matters where he listened and acted on her advice. Government plans to close hairdressing salons during the war were bad for morale, Eva argued, as men coming back from the Front would expect their womenfolk to look their best. Similarly, she argued that food rationing should be lightened or lifted for women whose men were home on leave, so they could enjoy a little pleasure from dining together.

And she openly disobeyed Hitler just once, when making the biggest decision of her life. Hitler had ordered her to stay in Bavaria, far from the dangers in Berlin. In early 1945 she spoke with Frau Linge, the wife of Hitler's valet, telling her that she had no intention of staying in the safety of Obersalzberg while he remained in the bomb-battered capital: 'Whatever happens I am returning to Berlin. If the Boss doesn't send for me within four weeks, I will go back on my own initiative. I am standing by him.'

And now in the early hours of 29 April she did stand by her new husband, getting married in circumstances that neither of them could have imagined in the distant days of the 1930s. After the ceremony was over, Heinz Linge congratulated her and was the first to call her Frau Hitler. The pleasure that this gave her was clear. She lived to enjoy the title for another 38 hours. The registrar, Walter Wagner, lasted a little longer. After a short drink and a few minutes of chat with the happy couple, he returned to his *Volkssturm* unit, now under fire at Potsdamer Platz. On 1 May he was killed by a Russian bullet through the head.

Chapter 3
Disintegration, 29 April, 11 a.m.

Hitler rose earlier than usual on the penultimate day of his life. Since his early days as a speaker in Munich, he had become accustomed to reading and working deep into the night, so it was normal for him to sleep late and have his breakfast when others around him were having lunch. Now there was so little time left, and so little for him to do, he had dressed himself by mid-morning and was already waiting for his valet to attend to him.

Heinz Linge was now more than a mere servant but had become the Führer's nurse by default. Just after 11 that morning Linge brought Hitler his accustomed light breakfast: normally tea and biscuits or a piece of sliced bread and an apple. He also brought pills for the stomach cramps that had bothered Hitler since his time in the trenches on the Western Front and gave him some eye drops containing a weak cocaine solution to ease an irritation in his right eye.

There was, however, a qualified SS doctor nearby, detailed to attend to Hitler's medical needs. Professor Werner Haase had first ministered to the Führer in 1935 and was much respected by Hitler for his surgical skills and his service as an SS medic at the Front. Haase was available in an emergency but was now spending almost all of his time over at the temporary operating theatre rigged up in the Reich Chancellery cellars, directing less qualified colleagues in the surgery of wounded men carried down from the chaotic street battles above. It was surgery that he could no longer perform himself, for he was seriously ill with tuberculosis and had been reduced to supervising operations from his couch for hours on end until he collapsed into sleep. As a result, the responsibility for ensuring that Hitler received his medication had devolved to the ever-reliable Linge.

The Führer drugged?

A supply of pills and other medication needed by the Führer had been left in the bunker when Hitler 'encouraged' his controversial physician, Dr Morell, to take a seat on one of the last flights out of Berlin, to Obersalzberg on 23 April. Although Hitler had often expressed his absolute faith in Morell, he now wanted to be rid of him. He feared that his favourite doctor might now be in league with Bormann and Goebbels. Both had repeatedly urged him to flee the capital for the relative safety of Bavaria but Hitler had just as repeatedly turned his face against quitting Berlin.

'How can I inspire the troops to battle for the city if I escape to a safe place?' he argued.

There was, of course, another key reason why Hitler was desperate to stay put. He understood that there was a far greater risk of being captured alive if he left the bunker, which would mean losing all control of his eventual fate. He would die in the bunker but at a time of his own choosing.

But if Morell sedated him, he might easily be transported to the Berghof against his will. Hitler was well aware that his two personal pilots, Hans Baur and Georg Betz, were both suspiciously lingering on in Berlin and there were still two reserve planes standing at Gatow Airport on the south-west side of the city. As a result, Morell had fallen victim to Hitler's paranoia.

It was the first time that Hitler had distrusted Morell since meeting him nine years before in 1936. Morell had gained some celebrity in 1930s Berlin attending to the needs, and pandering to the hypochondria, of a number of personalities in the city's theatrical and cinematic circles. These included Hitler's old friend and photographer Heinrich Hoffmann, who seems to have contracted gonorrhoea.

Dubious cures

Although he was a qualified medic who had served at the Front in the 1914–18 war, there was more than a hint of quackery about Morell, who treated his patients with his own dubious cures containing unknown quantities of vitamins and amphetamines. Morell's potions were also said to contain more unsavoury ingredients, such as extracts made from dung bacteria and from the semen and prostate glands of young bulls. Nevertheless, Hoffmann convinced Hitler to place his trust in the rather strange doctor.

During the intense crisis of the Austrian annexation and plebiscite in March and April 1938, an exhausted Hitler lost his voice after a particularly lengthy speech. While other physicians only offered rest as a solution, Morell offered him a concoction, probably containing an opiate, that soothed his damaged throat and allowed him to carry on campaigning. From then on, Morell was the first physician to the Führer.

Dr Theodor Morell was appointed Hitler's personal physician in 1937. Behind his back, he was nicknamed the 'Reich Master of Syringes' and is known to have prescribed a bizarre mixture of hard drugs and quack remedies for the Führer.

By the middle of the war, Hitler's doctor was regularly giving him injections of testosterone to boost his energy level, earning Morell the disparaging nickname among the Party leadership of 'Reich Master of Syringes'. Morell's records indicate that he administered 800 injections to Hitler in the years between 1942 and the end of the war. The chronicles also list a menu of 28 drugs including opiates, barbiturates and some toxins that Morell regularly dispensed to the Führer.

Pervitin

He also gave Hitler Pervitin, a combat stimulant based on methamphetamine that was distributed to front-line Wehrmacht troops and Luftwaffe pilots in the early years of the war. Nicknamed the 'Stuka Tablet', it allowed German troops to fight at high intensity for longer periods without needing sleep. Pervitin was also an 'ideologically sound' drug.

Before coming to power in 1933, the Nazis campaigned strongly against the illegal trade in cocaine and opium that had developed during the Weimar period, particularly in the larger, more liberal cities of Berlin and Hamburg. The drug trade was, in Nazi eyes, a key part of the Jewish conspiracy to weaken and control the German people. Pervitin, however, had been discovered by Fritz Hauschild, a German chemist working for the German pharmaceutical company Temmler, which was based in Berlin.

Almost 40 million Pervitin tablets were supplied to the German military in the Blitzkrieg War between 1939 and 1941. Even Erwin Rommel, the Panzer commander, used the drug to keep himself awake throughout critical periods during the invasions of Poland and France. However, the military use of the drug was officially discontinued when its side effects became apparent: after battle, troops who had taken Pervitin often suffered from serious exhaustion and prolonged periods of lethargy. Morell, however, continued to include small doses of Pervitin in the cocktail of pills and potions that he gave to the Führer.

Morell loathed by rivals

Other Nazi Party leaders did not share Hitler's trust in Morell and nor did the other leading medical men around the Führer, such as Karl Brandt, who now found themselves in Morell's shadow. They distrusted his methods and they were jealous of his proximity to power. He was also loathed for being a profiteer who had amassed a fortune after gaining exclusive rights to manufacture and supply some of his medical products to the German military. Every German soldier on the Eastern Front could testify to the fact that Morell's Russian Lice Powder was woefully ineffective.

Other critics simply believed that Morell's medicaments were contributing to the very clear deterioration in Hitler's health that became apparent in late 1942. Hitler had complained of several minor ailments before that year: pains in his back, stomach cramps and flatulence, trouble with his eyes (possibly a legacy of his being gassed in 1918) and several small polyps in his vocal chords that had to be removed. Also, after a major public speech he was almost always drenched in sweat, but this was understandable: his dramatic orations lasted two or more hours and involved a strenuous sequence of vigorous movements choreographed to convey his passion and dynamism.

Hitler's state of health

Despite this, Hitler had enjoyed relatively good health until his early 50s, perhaps because he had looked after himself. He never smoked and in fact he frowned upon smoking. Tobacco caused cancer, he believed: it damaged the heart and reduced lifespan. Ever the racial politician, he called tobacco 'the brown's man revenge' upon the white man, who had first introduced the coloured peoples to alcohol. He was a very moderate drinker himself, only occasionally having a small glass of schnapps or cognac in the late evenings with Eva, or while enjoying the hot baths that Linge prepared for him after an exhausting Party rally speech. Although he disliked the taste of wine, he sipped a little when required at public functions. He had drunk beer in his youth but in middle age he increasingly found it bitter and he gave it up completely in 1943 to keep his weight down.

His diet was always frugal and almost wholly vegetarian after 1937. He thought that meat-eating was unhealthy and avoided it throughout the last decade of his life. This might have been the result of his well-attested dislike of any form of cruelty to animals, including vivisection and the necessary techniques of the slaughterhouse. (Hitler's concern for other living creatures always presented a sharp contrast to his callous lack of concern for the millions of innocent people that were exterminated to bring about his social and political vision of the future.)

It may also have been a homage to his beloved Richard Wagner, who in later life had advocated vegetarianism as an aid to building a stronger German race.

Goebbels' propaganda machine presented Hitler's vegetarianism to the German people as evidence of their leader's iron will and self-discipline. Privately, however, Hitler continued to enjoy the Austrian liver-dumplings of his youth and he liked to consume the occasional sausage and bowl of turtle soup.

August Wollenhaupt, Hitler's personal barber from 1932 onwards, was better placed than most to observe the results of this abstemious lifestyle. He recorded that Hitler seemed fit and healthy into the early years of the war, his skin staying fair and unblemished, his hair remaining fine and soft, his eyes still bright and attractive. In appearance, Hitler was always smart and very well-groomed, he said. Wollenhaupt last cut Hitler's hair in early March 1945 but the Hitler he saw at this last appointment was a very different man: 'He was visibly trembling, old, a shell of what he had once been, he was the walking dead.'

General Weidling, the last commander of the German forces defending Berlin, met Hitler several times in the final weeks of the war. He later described the physical wreck that Hitler had become by that stage: his skin was pallid and bloated, his eyes were puffy and feverish and his left leg constantly shuddered. Both of his hands trembled and he struggled with uncontrollable tremors throughout his left arm. There were also several obvious food stains on the clothes of this once immaculate man.

Shocked at his appearance

Armin Lehmann was a fervent 16-year-old member of the Hitler Youth who in late April 1945 was serving in the *Volkssturm* as a runner carrying messages across the battlefield that was central Berlin. He was selected as one of the birthday honour guard to be reviewed by Hitler in the Reich Chancellery garden on 20 April. In later life he remembered the disappointment he had felt as the Führer shuffled down the line towards him. He could not believe that 'this withered old man in front of me was the visionary who had led our nation to greatness'.

New visitors to the Führerbunker were forewarned not to expect to see the potent figure portrayed in countless newsreels and on front pages back in the 1930s. Despite the warning, though, they were invariably shocked. Since 1942, Hitler had made very few appearances in public, so his cinema presence increasingly depended upon old footage from much earlier times. As a result, this hunched old man who looked a decade more than his age was not the leader they expected. The Führer had been ill, they were told, and had worn himself out expending every ounce of energy on protecting the German people. The more perceptive visitors noticed that the chill fire in his bright blue eyes, which had entranced all those who fell under his spell, had gone out.

Hitler's deterioration was clear to all who worked with him. The massive scale of defeat at Stalingrad in terms of men and machinery had deeply punctured the German public's faith in Hitler and the Nazi Party. It had also undermined Hitler's self-confidence in his ability to carry out his self-proclaimed national mission. The tremor in his left arm was first noticed at this point, even though he tried to hide it by using his other arm as a brace.

Some blamed his physical decline on the bomb blast on 20 July 1944, yet he had quickly shrugged off the wounds to his leg and was well enough to meet Mussolini later that same day and walk with him in the forest around the Wolf's Lair compound. Nevertheless, in some respects he was deeply affected by the explosion. After the bomb, it was noted that his usually intense concentration during strategic discussions had begun to weaken and his grasp of detail had started to loosen. He also seemed more easily distracted at times throughout the late summer campaign, at a crucial point in the war when he now faced the growing Allied legions in western and southern France, in addition to the Soviet steamroller lumbering remorselessly westwards.

Morell's treatments suspected

Some of the senior medical staff involved in Hitler's care suspected that Morell's unconventional treatments were the primary cause of his physical decline. Dr Erwin Giesing, a member of the NSDAP and a decorated military doctor, was summoned to the Wolf's Lair after the 20 July bomb blast. He was struck by the contrast between the masterful Führer of old and the prematurely ageing patient now lying before him on the examination table: an 'almost depleted and exhausted man trying to keep going on the vestiges of his strength'. More than 200 wooden splinters had already been removed from Hitler's legs by another physician, Hanskarl von Hasselbach.

Giesing, however, was an ear specialist called upon to treat the damage done to Hitler's eardrums by the force of the blast, which he did with some success thanks to repeated swabbing with a solution containing cocaine. When Giesing was summoned again in the autumn to treat Hitler for jaundice, he began to suspect that he was being poisoned by Morell's unorthodox medicines.

He tested one of those that Hitler had long been taking in large quantities: Dr Koester's Anti-Gas Pills. After swallowing one of these, Giesing felt distinctly ill. Chemical analysis revealed that the pills contained a small amount of strychnine. They also contained atropine, a hallucinogen in small quantities but a poison when overdosed. Around the same period Himmler had another of Morell's compounds analysed. It was mostly amphetamine. Yet when these discoveries were brought to Hitler's attention, he dismissed his suspicious medics (Brandt, von Hasselbach and Giesing) and retained Morell. He knew which doctor could be bullied into giving him the powerful remedies that his frail body now needed: drugs that would relieve his pains and help him cope with the stress of command as the Allies closed in for the kill.

Troglodyte existence

Hitler's health was not helped by the troglodyte existence he had maintained for much of the last three years of the war. Apart from some relatively brief periods of respite at the Berghof, from the beginning of 1942 onwards he spent most of his time, approximately 1,100 days, in one or other of his numerous underground command posts scattered around the edges of his empire. The German public were told little about his whereabouts. Goebbels had in fact taken on the public morale-boosting duties that Churchill had undertaken during the Blitz in England – visiting the survivors of bombing raids and posing with the plucky wounded in hospitals – while Hitler largely disappeared from public view and went underground.

At Wolffschanze in East Prussia and Werwolf in Western Ukraine there were some fleeting opportunities to catch a little fresh air at moments of calm. Visits to military posts nearer the front line also gave Hitler a chance to fill his lungs and feel the sunlight on his face. After he entered the Führerbunker on 16 January 1945, however, he seldom emerged from the concrete and saw little of the outside world above ground again. By April, conditions in the bunker were distinctly insanitary; plumbing difficulties and the chaos of those last weeks had resulted in uncollected waste in the latrines and the rancid stench of stale urine began to permeate the bunker corridors. Although the generator barely managed to supply enough electricity to produce a dim, flickering light in the rooms, it effortlessly provided a constant drumming reverberation and a noxious reek of diesel fumes. Three years of subterranean life in conditions such as these had taken a very heavy toll on Hitler's physical and emotional health and had sapped his strength.

Last public appearance

On 15 March, he asked his chauffeur Kempka to drive him to the Front, then near Frankfurt an der Oder, about an hour east of Berlin. Along the route, Hitler's car was mobbed by ecstatic locals. He waved, smiled, shook their outstretched hands and spoke to all the troops or farmers and their families that recognized him. Despite his grey hair and hunched bearing, they were once more entranced by the sheer force of his personality. His sudden presence among them, so close to the dangers that they faced, gave them renewed hope. For a few moments, they forgot about the massed Russian battalions only a few miles away. Now they believed once again that 'the Führer would find a way'.

But Hitler was utterly exhausted by the effort of recreating the old vision of himself. Completely drained, he sank back quietly into his seat beside Kempka and ordered him to drive back to Berlin as quickly as possible. It was the sly old dictator's last performance. Like all of his public appearances from the earliest days in Munich's Hofbrauhaus onwards, it was a carefully calculated and well-rehearsed piece of theatre. Over the years, he had spent hours in front of a mirror, practising every gesture, every facial expression, even being photographed doing so by Heinrich Hoffmann, his photographer. But now there was nothing left in the tank. From that day until his death, Hitler remained in his bunker.

Final weeks in the bunker

The staff who remained with him in the Führerbunker during the final weeks had maintained a surprisingly high standard of self-discipline. Even in the last week of April, with the Russians only a few hundred metres away, the bunker staff tried to busy themselves with their duties, no matter how pointless they had become. The secretaries sat at their desks typing orders and messages that would never reach their recipients and the radio operators waited for signals that were no longer coming in.

As late as 23 April, there had still been men able and willing to take the risk of going up into the maelstrom above to repair damaged cables: now there was no one. The internal telephone system between the bunker and the Reich Chancellery had also broken down and there was no one to repair that either. Orders for General Wenck, who commanded the largest functioning army unit near Berlin, had to be sent by two motorcyclists. One was captured by German troops who believed he was a spy: the other simply disappeared. Finally, the air balloon that conveyed radio signals in and out of Berlin was destroyed on the morning of 29 April, effectively cutting the bunker off from what remained of the Third Reich.

Fear of death

For the bunkerites, there was no longer anything to be done except wait for the end and hope for a chance to escape. Although every one of them considered the war lost and feared that their own fate was sealed, they continued to treat the Führer with the utmost respect. Yet as Kempka noted: 'Though everybody male and female was making the effort to remain composed, the inner nervousness of all was obvious.' Some resorted to the bottle for support. Generals Krebs and Burgdorf were slumped in the sofas in the bunker corridor while slowly inebriating themselves and even stolid Bormann had taken a few glasses to steady himself. Eva sipped a schnapps or two to help the time pass.

Linge later insisted that while Hitler lived everyone acted with restraint and that any drinking that took place was done in moderation. But Linge spent most of his time in the Führerbunker. A hundred metres or so away in the Reich Chancellery, the inhabitants of its tunnels and cellars awaited the arrival of the Russians in a much more uninhibited way.

The Chancellery cellars hosted the last surviving bakery in Berlin and in them were stored ample supplies of smoked beef, salami, pickles and cheese. They also held vast quantities of alcohol. There were several hundred Germans in the cellars throughout the last hours of April 1945 and most of them were young. There was dancing, heavy drinking and, inevitably, debauchery. As in all wars, the imminence of death loosened social restraints and encouraged the impulse to indulge in casual but life-affirming copulation.

A CITY UNDER SIEGE

Debauchery

These same urges swept across the city. Drunks could be found imbibing in the ruined streets, sitting on the rubble of a collapsed house or leaning against a small pile of dead combatants, oblivious to the Soviet shells landing around them. Other Berliners were desperate to be close to other living beings while still alive. The Danish correspondent Jacob Kronika witnessed the collapse of normal social proprieties in those last days in April before the Red Army arrived. At night, large numbers of men and women sought each other out in the public parks for uninhibited and often public erotic encounters. Many were very young people in uniform. Kronika noted: 'A frantic lust has been released during the downfall of Berlin. We want to do everything because we might be killed tonight or tomorrow, that seems to be the motto these days.'

Food and water shortages

Finding food and water was also becoming a serious problem for many Berliners. As recently as 22 April, Goebbels had declared that there were sufficient supplies of tinned foods and sugar in the city, but in a large metropolitan area such as Berlin the availability of food differed from area to area and from family to family. On 27 April, the Nazi authorities were still distributing some food to selected suburbs. However, the situation had clearly deteriorated in many parts of the city. Water was scarce in a number of places and there were long queues at the water pumps that were still operating. The authorities had posted a regulation banning the use of water for bathing and showering but their effort was quite unnecessary. Every Berliner already knew well enough that they had only enough to drink and none to waste on worrying about body odour.

And the Berliners in the long queues outside food stores were certainly hungry enough to run the risk of being caught in a Russian bombardment. After months of tight rationing and the collapse of the food distribution system, the streets of Berlin were now witness to scenes of medieval horror. Armin Lehmann, the Hitler Youth courier, never forgot the sound of a shrieking horse that had been badly wounded by shrapnel. The two hungry men who found the horse had no ammunition to kill it, so they butchered it live with a saw and a knife. Then on 30 April a large white ox was found wandering in the streets. It was led away and slaughtered in a nearby courtyard, where a vicious fight with knives and metal buckets broke out among its butchers, all determined to hack out their share of its carcass and its blood.

At night, the very hungry took the risk of climbing out from their shelters in search of food. They looked for army rations in the pockets and kitbags of the thousands of dead soldiers who littered the streets of Berlin. Others broke into ruined shops and houses in defiance of the Nazi prohibition on looting. Some were inevitably caught and in time-honoured fashion they were executed and left hanging at prominent street junctions as a warning to others.

Infrastructure smashed

By the end of April, two weeks of constant and massive Russian artillery bombardment had smashed most of the bits of Berlin's infrastructure that had survived three years of American and British aerial bombing. Much of the city was without gas and electricity and the remaining water was strictly rationed. Little remained of the transport network: 90 of the railway and underground stations in the Berlin urban area had been damaged or were now flooded. There were also few cars left in Berlin, other than the dozens of burned-out relics that had been shoved to the side of the roads. Those cars that were still fit to drive had to be driven at high speed in a weave pattern to have any chance of avoiding the Ilyushin Shturmovik fighters that dominated the skies above the city. But driving at speed along Berlin's deeply cratered roads offered its own dangers.

Around 50,000 buildings had been totally destroyed and many more had been badly damaged. They had been reduced to an estimated 70 million tons of rubble. The devastation across much of the inner city would only be equalled by that of Hiroshima and Nagasaki, two months later. Most of the buildings in the central government quarter had simply collapsed under the weight of the Soviet bombardment.

Those who witnessed the hellishness of Berlin at the end of April, like Hitler's Luftwaffe adjutant Nicolaus von Below, who emerged from the bunker on 30 April, spoke of an inferno rather than a city: the confusion of tram wires, tram lines and telegraph wires wrapped around and within a desert of rubble and dust, the bomb craters filling with a noxious brown-green fluid, the fires raging on the horizon

A Russian patrol fights its way through the rubble in the Steglitz district of Berlin, 24 April 1945.

in all directions, the sky obscured with dense cloud, the air thick with a vicious phosphorus smoke laden with the smack of diesel and the sickly-sweet stench of the scorched dead, both equine and human, lying in the streets.

Death from the air

The number of Berliners and others killed in the Battle for Berlin can never be known with certainty. Many Berliners had fled to hopefully safer places in the countryside, but their place had been taken by the long columns of refugees from East Prussia, Brandenburg and Silesia that had flooded into the city since the start of the year. Some idea of the impact of the war on Hitler's capital can be gauged by the stark fact that in 1939 the city was home to 4.3 million inhabitants and by 1946 that figure had dropped to under

2.8 million. The number of civilian dead was swollen by the increased aerial attacks in the latter months of the war when the USAF and Bomber Command of the RAF were joined by the Soviet Air Force and the French Armée de l'Air.

On the ground, the Nazi authorities were also struggling to maintain their previously well-organized air raid service. Many of its volunteers were now wearing the armband of the *Volkssturm* and were engaged elsewhere in direct combat with the enemy. Erich Kempka and his colleagues spent their nights assisting the fire brigade to put out fires and to find victims trapped in burning and collapsed buildings. With limited numbers of helpers, their duties became more arduous every night.

Civilians in the deeper bunkers were relatively safe and they had developed the same kind of cheery and defiant, if sometimes grisly, morale that had characterized the earlier British response to aerial bombing. But if shelters nearer the surface suffered too many direct hits and collapsed, there were now fewer hands to clear away the rubble and rescue any survivors. One Scandinavian observer estimated that many thousands of Berliners died underground, trapped by falling masonry and left to die of thirst and starvation.

War-weary Germans

Nor was there time to even bury the dead, as the intrepid American journalist Virginia Irwin discovered when she entered outer Berlin on 27 April; she found 'a city of the dead' with German corpses piled up on the pavements and in the front gardens of suburban bomb-shattered homes. The systematic cleansing of the city would only really begin in May, with the conscription of all women between 15 and 65 as *Trümmerfrauen* or rubble-women.

Among the rubble and the dead were countless copies of *Mein Kampf* and images of the Führer. Allegiance to the Nazi regime was evaporating in this new reality of a soon-to-be conquered city. Goebbels knew better than anyone else in the Reich how deep public disenchantment with National Socialism now ran. Throughout the 13 years of Nazi rule, his spies from the Ministry of Propaganda and Public Enlightenment had been monitoring the chat and humour in the cafés and streets of Germany in order to gauge public morale.

But despite his best efforts to maintain enthusiasm for the cause, Goebbels knew that the Germans were war weary. Most of them had accepted some time before that the war was inevitably lost and that the Hitler Age was now coming to an end. The *Hakenkreuz*, or swastika, began to disappear from daily life and copies of books, pamphlets, uniforms, photographs and any other Nazi paraphernalia were hidden or burned.

Disintegration of the Nazi Party

Members of the Waffen SS were to regret the one memory of Nazism that could not be easily erased; the obligatory SS blood tattoo high on their left arm. If they were captured by the Russians, discovery of the tattoo meant summary execution or, worse, a long slow death in a Soviet punishment camp. Should they be apprehended by the Western Allies, it meant probable prosecution as an accessory to the hideous war crimes committed by the SS throughout eastern Europe. However, for most Germans the Nazi Party, the movement

Reichsminister of Propaganda Joseph Goebbels and his wife Magda stayed with Hitler until the bitter end – this involved arranging the murder of their six children in the bunker.

that was the bedrock of Hitler's One-Thousand Year Reich, was already on its way into the dustbin of history.

The Party had been disintegrating since January, if not before, and it did not help when the regional governors of Nazi Germany, the Gauleiters, met with the Führer at the start of 1945. Few of them had seen Hitler in recent years as most of his time had been spent deep in occupied territory near to the Eastern Front, so they had largely been left to govern their own provinces as they saw fit and with little direction from central government. Many were shocked by his physical condition and by how quickly he had aged. His speech that day was a rehash of his eternal themes. They had heard it all before many times and had usually been reinspired by it, but this time it had fallen flat, not least because of Hitler's weak and listless delivery.

It was a dispiriting and demoralizing signal to send out to a group of men who owed their power and authority to the Führer and who were vital to maintaining the national war effort. On 30 January, Hitler made a radio broadcast to the nation to mark the 12th year of the Third Reich. It was a serious mistake. Goebbels' spies reported that listeners were not only stunned but frightened by how tired and dulled-down the Führer sounded. For them, the reassuring belief in their strong, tireless leader had evaporated. Goebbels learned the lesson and ensured that it was Hitler's final message to his people.

Blind obedience to the Nazi Party had taken another blow following the Battle of Aachen in October 1944. The fighting for Charlemagne's city lasted for 19 days and the Wehrmacht defended it tenaciously, so much so that the Americans suffered heavy casualties, with over 5,000 killed or wounded. Despite this, when the US forces entered the city they generally acted with disciplined restraint towards those remaining inhabitants who had not been evacuated by the Nazi authorities. Nor did they raze Aachen, a city of great cultural riches and historic symbolism, as some Nazi propaganda had predicted.

White flags of surrender

Millions of war-weary Germans took note: regardless of Goebbels' warnings, they could expect decent treatment from the Western Allies. As Allied troops advanced in the following spring, many white flags of surrender appeared in towns and villages throughout western Germany. Citizens had to take great care with their timing when hanging out their white sheets, however, for there were armed Nazi fanatics in every community. Goebbels had repeatedly called upon every loyal German to cleanse the Reich of 'this plague bacteria' of white flags.

Regional Party officials had explicit instructions from Berlin to execute any families displaying signs of surrender and they had been similarly ordered to liquidate any local officials who liaised with Allied commanders. This was no idle threat and the order was carried out in numerous locations throughout the Reich. Many families who raised the white flag a little too soon before the Allies arrived were eliminated for defeatism and treason. The new mayor of Aachen, Franz Oppenhoff, appointed by the Americans, was assassinated in March 1945 by order of Himmler himself and defeatist officials in several Bavarian towns were also shot or hanged by the SS before they could surrender to the Americans.

As a result of these demonstrations of lingering loyalty to Nazism, Allied strategists feared a long, lingering guerrilla war against the Werewolves: groups of trained and well-armed Nazi loyalists scattered throughout Austria and Germany. Yet in the last days of April, whatever enthusiasm for National Socialism still existed in Germany was dissipating very rapidly. Changes in the graffiti adorning the walls of Berlin heralded a change of political direction.

There were still many examples of the optimistically defiant *Berlin bleibt deutsch*, Berlin stays German. But now openly anti-Nazi slogans were appearing: Against SS Traitors and Death to the War Extenders! A small group of armed German Communists had even opened fire upon SS units near Hermannplatz in the leftist district of Neukölln. And one astute witness saw a potent sign in the heart of the Führerbunker itself which showed that Hitler's authority was now slipping away completely. A thick cloud of malodorous cigarette smoke hung in the air where a group of bunkerites had gathered. They were openly smoking in the corridor outside Hitler's room. It was clear that Hitler had lost the power to command and that the Third Reich was already finished.

Chapter 4
Terror and Revenge, 29 April, 2 p.m.

Suicide discussion

At around 2 p.m. on 29 April Hitler sat down with Eva and the secretaries for a light lunch. He preferred to eat with the female bunkerites and usually liked to talk about things that had nothing to do with their present predicament. Often the chat was about his German shepherd Blondi and her pups. Today he surprised his tablemates by launching into a discussion about the best way to commit suicide. After reflection, Hitler expressed his preference for the pistol rather than for poison. The bullet smashed into the skull so quickly that death was instantaneous. He had seen many deaths of that kind in the 1914–18 war and knew that a bullet offered a quick and efficient way to die.

Eva disagreed and showed Traudl Junge and Gerda Christian the phial of prussic acid that she carried in the pocket of her dress. She was worried that she would make a mess of shooting herself and might damage her face, because she wanted to look beautiful even in death. And besides, the doctors had assured her that prussic acid was also very quick and quite painless. This gruesome conversation didn't put the secretaries off their lunch. Instead, they listened to every word intently and pondered them deeply. They too had poison capsules, a gift from Hitler several days before. And both women were trying to summon up the courage to use them before the Russians came.

Heinrici's last stand

The Red Army reached the capital of the Reich much sooner than most Berliners expected. At the start of 1945 the war had still seemed far away in eastern Poland. Yet in little more than three weeks the Front had moved at a frightening pace, from the Vistula in central Poland to the very border of the Reich along the river Oder. By early February much of the Soviet line was only a short morning's drive from the centre of the German capital. At that point, Stalin ordered his generals to rest and re-equip their forces while the remaining isolated German units in East Prussia and Pomerania were picked off one by one. It was only a matter of time before the Battle for Berlin would commence and then be brought to an inevitably victorious conclusion by the vastly superior Soviet armed forces.

The German commander, General Gotthard Heinrici, chose to make his stand at the Seelow Heights, a raised bluff overlooking the Oder river and its floodplain, 55 miles (88 km) east of Berlin. Along much of the Front the Germans were outnumbered in terms of men by almost ten to one, and they were seriously outgunned. However, Heinrici was an experienced defensive commander. He ordered his engineers to create three fortified lines of anti-tank ditches and gun emplacements overlooking the Russians on the flat land below. And he opened the local reservoirs to create a marshy quagmire below his emplacements, to slow down the approaching enemy.

Berlin bombarded

The final major Russian advance towards Berlin began at Seelow on 16 April. Almost a million Soviet troops, supported by a vast armada of tanks and mobile artillery, advanced towards the entrenched German position and some of the most bitter fighting of the entire war. It took three days and 30,000 casualties for the Red Army to eventually make its superior resources count but the Seelow Heights, long nicknamed the 'Gates of Berlin', had been taken. There was now no further serious defensive obstacle ahead of them. On 21 April, Soviet artillery was arrayed just outside the suburbs of the city and began to strike at its heart. The Soviet bombardment continued for the next 11 days without cessation until the city was captured.

Carnage at Karstadt

Long queues of civilians, snatching a last chance to see if there were any precious food supplies left in the giant Karstadt store on Hermannplatz, were the first to learn that central Berlin was now in the front line. A salvo of Russian shells pulverized dozens of waiting shoppers and the horror of the scene terrified the survivors and those deployed to clear away the carnage. This first demonstration of the power of the Red Army made a deep impression on men and women who were no strangers to modern war and who had already quite bravely withstood several years of aerial bombing.

On 24 April, Russian artillery shelling penetrated the underground motor garage that was part of the Reich Chancellery and bunker complex. The roof of the deep Führerbunker nearby withstood the onslaught but the

The famous Karstadt department store on Hermannplatz was practically wiped off the map by the Russian bombardment in 1945.

constant sound of Russian bombardment added to the persistent dread and tension felt by its inhabitants.

Living corpses

Working at the centre of what remained of the Reich's communication and command network, the inhabitants of the Führerbunker well understood how close the Russians now were, how few resources were left to resist them and how little time remained before the city fell. The bunkerites responded to their grim situation with gallows humour. They nicknamed their subterranean home 'the funeral parlour' and called themselves 'the living corpses'. But even the most loyal admirers of the Führer were torn between their sense of loyalty to the Boss and their desperate hope that they would have just enough time to escape from the bunker before the Reds arrived.

Conversations inevitably turned to the key question on everyone's mind: how to survive and what would happen to them when the Bolshevik barbarians arrived. The women who remained with Hitler in the bunker thought and spoke of little else in these last days of the war. Like thousands of women in the city above, Hitler's female staff worried about 'it': the moment when they would be at the mercy of the brutal Soviet hordes. His secretaries wanted to be ready for 'the ultimate eventuality'.

It was known that Hitler had a cache of poison capsules, cyanide or prussic acid, some supplied to him by Himmler and others from his personal physician, Dr Morell. On 26 April, some of the secretaries had asked for, and were given, a useful parting gift from their Führer. The terror that paralyzed them, and so many other female Berliners, was fuelled by the tales of Soviet brutality spread by the columns of refugees fleeing from the eastern provinces of the Reich. And thanks to Goebbels' propaganda ministry the name of one Soviet atrocity was on everyone's lips: Nemmersdorf.

Nemmersdorf massacre

On 21 October 1944, an advance Soviet tank brigade with support infantry had briefly occupied the East Prussian farming village of Nemmersdorf, about 40 km (25 miles) inside the border of the Reich. The Germans hurled everything available at the invaders, forcing them to withdraw the following day. The inhabitants of Nemmersdorf had not been treated well by the Red Army troops who had temporarily taken control of their village.

A German military situation report noted that 26 inhabitants, mostly old people, had been killed and two local women had been raped. Generaloberst Reinhardt, then commander of the Wehrmacht's Army Group Centre, visited the area and confirmed that some women in the village had been violated by Red Army troops. He said little more about the incident. As a Panzer Corps commander in the East since 1941, he was doubtless inured to the horrors of war.

It was left to the staff from Goebbels' propaganda ministry to sear the name of Nemmersdorf into the minds of the German public. The newsreel they produced contained graphic images of rows of infant corpses, their heads apparently smashed open by the rifle butts of Soviet infantrymen.

Now it seemed that more than 60 women in the village had been raped and in many cases mutilated and murdered by the Reds. And it was claimed that German women had been stripped naked and crucified on the doors of their farmhouses and barns.

The newsreel had the exact effect that Goebbels intended. It terrified German cinema-goers and confirmed long-standing Nazi claims that the Slavic and Asiatic hordes from the East were subhuman brutes, *Untermenschen*. The German people were reminded that they were engaged in a war for their very survival.

Every citizen of the Reich would have to strain their utmost in this total war or the nation would be destroyed. There was a surge of volunteers for the *Volkssturm*.

Fall of Königsberg

Tales of the fall of Königsberg, the main city of East Prussia, on 9 April left Berliners in no doubt about what would happen to them when their city was inevitably captured. Hans von Lehndorf, chief doctor at a hospital in Königsberg, was present when the Russians arrived at his institute and gang-raped their way through all the available females, both nurses and patients. In his memoirs, he wrote of the difficulty of describing the horrors he had witnessed: 'This is man without God ... the most terrible thing that exists among men.'

Otto Lasch, a blunt soldier and commander of Königsberg during the last six months of the war, eventually gave a fuller report of what he saw as he marched out of the city with his surviving men into a decade of imprisonment in a Soviet prison camp. He described scenes that were straight from a medieval depiction of hell:

> Houses burned and smoked. Everything in them thrown out on the streets. Smashed vehicles stood between burning tanks, clothing, equipment everywhere. Among the debris, drunken Russians danced and fired off out of control, searching for girls and women who were dragged into the houses despite trying to resist. Corpses filled the ditches at the side of the streets. Many of them were badly damaged and the dead women had clearly been raped: bodies dangled from trees, dead children lay around in large numbers. Stupefied, benumbed German women were led in all directions, drunken Russians flogged a German nun, women came out of the houses,

hands raised imploringly: the Russians chased them back in and shot them if they didn't hurry. We had never imagined such things.

Polish troops fighting in the Red Army were especially vicious as they took their chance to mete out revenge for the appalling atrocities their people had suffered from 1939 onwards. Königsberg suffered badly – partly because of the stubborn resistance of its defenders, which had cost the Red Army many casualties, and partly because it was the first major German settlement to fall into Soviet hands. But Königsberg had also for centuries been a powerful symbol of Teutonic mastery over the native peoples of Eastern Europe. Now the Slav had the upper hand.

As citizens of the Reich's capital, Berliners knew that they would suffer an even more dreadful retribution, because their city was, in the jargon of Soviet propaganda, the viper's nest, Hitler's lair.

Soviets enter Berlin

On 23 April, Soviet infantry assault groups supported by artillery, tanks and flamethrower specialists began to penetrate the suburbs of Berlin. It was soon clear to them that the city was ill defended since the German commanders had gambled most of their remaining resources on stopping the Red Army at Seelow and other defensive points far from the city. Within twenty-four hours, Soviet troops advancing from the south-east were making headway through the German defences along the southern S-bahn line and had crossed the Teltow Canal south of Neukölln.

Despite ferocious close combat and grim house-to-house operations, large parts of the outer suburbs in southern and south-eastern Berlin were in Soviet hands by dawn on 26 April. As the fighting closed in on the centre of the city and 'the Citadel', the hopeful name given to the government quarter, thousands of Soviet troops were now beginning to enjoy their control over the city's civilian population.

Berliners later noted that the *Frontviki* usually wanted practical things: food, water and information about German snipers or troops armed with deadly tank-busting *Panzerfauste* and *Panzerschrecke*. At most, they generally helped themselves to some small valuables such as watches and jewellery. It was usually the second-line troops that followed who had the time to loot and abuse the population at their leisure.

Berliners soon witnessed the casual way in which Soviet troops shot civilians who protested their actions or merely dithered when given instructions. Men in any kind of uniform, not just Nazi Party members but civic functionaries such as firemen, police and even postmen, ran the risk of instant execution. In the chaos of those days and nights in late April and early May 1945, no one was counting the dead, but later estimates suggested that well over 100,000 East Prussian and Berlin male civilians were simply gunned down in their homes and the streets while their farms and shops were put to the torch.

Outraged by German prosperity

The very obvious prosperity of their hated enemy outraged and often bewildered the Russian invaders, who now found themselves in a land of unimaginable plenty. The wealth to be found in the mansions of the Prussian Junkers class was understandable: after all they were, according to Soviet Marxist propaganda, rapacious aristocrats who had lived off the labour of their serfs for generations. The comfortable homes of the prosperous bourgeoisie also made sense. They too had done well from the unjust capitalist system.

It was the standard of living of much of the German working class that perplexed many Soviet soldiers. They had been told since the Bolshevik Revolution in 1917 that working folk in the West were mercilessly exploited and crushed by their economic overlords. But now they found that many ordinary Germans lived in well-built and well-equipped homes that they could only dream of back in the Soviet Motherland. Most ordinary working-class Germans enjoyed luxuries such as clean running water, efficient drainage and gas and electrical supplies that often still worked after six years of war. In many cases, their larders were still well-stocked and their cupboards were full of well-laundered linen; wardrobes revealed a choice of good-quality clothing and shoes.

Before the war, Germans of quite modest means had clearly had the money to equip and adorn their homes to a good standard, many owning pieces of quality furniture, glassware and ceramics. Here was the evidence that even the workers of Germany were capitalists as well as fascists. Everywhere there was evidence of the superiority of the German economy and of the high cultural aspirations and interests of many German families, hence the glee with which Soviet soldiers stole or just smashed symbols of German intellectual attainment.

Books and paintings were thrown out of windows into the streets and burned if they had no obvious monetary value or could not be siphoned back home to Russia. Pianos were a particularly vulnerable symbol of German bourgeois affluence and many met an inglorious and discordant end. The destruction of a particularly fine vintage harpsichord, thrown from a high-storied building on to the cobbled streets of Leignitz in Lower Silesia, represents whole orchestras of musical instruments that were victims of proletarian fury. Time and again Russian soldiers who were astonished by the evidence of German prosperity asked themselves: 'Why did these educated people who had so much and who were living so well want to invade our impoverished land?'

Rape by the Soviets

The population of Berlin was now about to suffer from the toxic mixture of war-weariness, rage, jealousy and revenge that engulfed much of the Red Army. Berlin's women took the brunt. Later estimates suggested that somewhere between 110,000 and 130,000 Berlin women and girls were raped during and immediately after the two-week Battle for Berlin. The many victims and witnesses who later wrote of what has been called 'the biggest mass rape in history' tell the same sad tales: the rape of females of all ages from young girls to old matrons; the repeated gang rape of one or two women, often mother and daughter or sisters, by large numbers of troops; the public nature of many gang rapes; the rape of nuns and of nurses and patients in hospitals – the gang rapes at the maternity hospital at Dahlem in the south-west of the city were a particularly savage outrage; the rape of women in front of their families and especially their husbands and other menfolk; and the frequent beatings, butchery and slaughter of raped women. Husbands, fathers and sons who tried to protect their womenfolk were simply gunned down.

Women who had reason to welcome the arrival of the Soviets and to expect better treatment from the conquerors were quickly disappointed and dismayed. The wives of Communist and Socialist sympathizers who had long suffered under the Nazis; the Jewish women and girls who were 'liberated' at the Schulstrasse transit camp to the north-west of the city centre; the large numbers of young women abducted from Russia, Poland, Romania, Hungary and the Baltic lands and taken to Germany to work as slave labourers; all were equal prey in the eyes of the Red Army.

For more than two weeks there was no law in the city. Public gang rape was so common that it prompted a jibe about the Soviet communist system that was attributed to the Soviet film director Agranenko but ruefully passed on by Berliners: 'Red Army soldiers do not commit to individual relationships: as good Communists they rape on a collective basis.'

One woman bravely complained to a Soviet commander that she had been repeatedly violated by his men, but he casually dismissed the matter: his men had not done her any real harm and, besides, all of his men were healthy. Sadly, he was almost certainly mistaken. Records show that around 10,000 Berlin women were infected by their rapists and had to face the continuing trauma of syphilis and/or gonorrhoea in a city without antibiotics.

Avoiding attack

Women did what they could to avoid their fate by appearing older and unattractive: wearing dirty clothes that aged them; cutting their hair; covering their faces with filthy hats; and removing false teeth to draw in and age their faces. Some dressed as men and others only left their homes accompanied by small children at their side, as acts of kindness to small children by homesick Russian troops had been observed. Where possible, women tried to establish an exclusive, intimate relationship with a Red Army officer to escape the attentions of his men: 'Better a Russian on your belly than a bullet in your head' was the bitter slogan of the day.

They quickly learned that the safest time to venture out for food, water or help was in the early morning hours before dawn, when the Russian soldiers were still sleeping off the alcohol and debauchery of the previous night. The danger time was just after nightfall when organized 'hunting packs' armed with torches and guns searched for women in what remained of Berlin's housing stock. There were many cases where well-hidden daughters were instantly found and dragged out of their hiding holes: frightened neighbours had given their location away to the Russians in the hope of diverting attention away from their own women. As few glass windows had survived the incessant bombardment of the city by Western aircraft and Soviet artillery, the screams and the weeping could be heard in every corner of the city throughout the long nights.

Suicide and shame

After the initial shock, many women accepted their fate and realized that their best chance of survival lay in calmly obeying the command '*Frau komm*'. Those who resisted were more likely to be beaten, or worse. Many learned to blank out the experience and then repress it while others talked and laughed ruefully about the rapes in an attempt to shrug off their memories. However, many women simply

The streets to the Reich Chancellery are lined with mangled German vehicles as Russian soldiers back a lorry up to the main entrance and take away a looted stone eagle with swastika.

could not come to terms with what had happened to them. Estimates suggest that a very high percentage of the 10,000 or so female corpses that passed through the city morgues that summer were suicides.

Some entire families destroyed themselves by hanging or poison rather than endure the shame of having had a wife or daughter violated. A large number of women rejected their husbands and boyfriends and avoided all future sexual contact. Many men felt deeply unmanned by their inability to protect their women and couldn't bear to think or hear about what had happened. Others were embittered when women began to try and laugh off their experience. It was not uncommon for men to break off an engagement with a raped fiancée or abandon a raped wife. The aftermath of those final weeks of the war hung over Berlin for many months to come: the abortion clinics were busy throughout the summer and the 'occupation children' began to arrive in the early months of winter. Then came the problem of dealing with the rush of abandoned babies.

Rape by other nations

All conquering armies loot and rape: to the victor the spoils. British, American and French troops also committed atrocities against German women as they fought their way into the Western Reich. French soldiers in particular committed a number of outrages in south-western Germany, notably at Freiburg and some of the towns near Lake Constance. The French Command excused these incidents by saying that they had mostly been committed by poorly disciplined colonial troops, tough mountain fighters from Morocco who expected to loot and pillage their defeated enemies by right.

The treatment of German civilians by British and American troops varied from unit to unit and often depended upon the attitude of local Allied commanders. A correspondent with Patton's Third Army noted in April 1945 that 'after the fighting moved on to German soil, there was a good deal of rape by combat troops and those immediately following them'. A large number of abortions were carried out after American units occupied Berchtesgaden, the symbolic home of the Führer. Most American units behaved well towards the defeated but more than 400 US troops stood trial for rape in the spring of 1945 and 45 of these were sentenced to periods of hard labour.

British troops were known to have raped at Neustadt am Rübenberge and in the Nienburg area and several British padres expressed their concern at the way many infantrymen treated German women in captured settlements, particularly in the first hours after a tough military engagement. However, once the blood had cooled it was not uncommon for American and British servicemen to excuse their rough behaviour by leaving the women some goods or money as compensation, as if rewarding a prostitute. There were also complaints by a number of German families, who reported that British troops billeted upon them had sexually interfered with their children.

In 1946 one candid US officer described the impact of alcohol on war-weary young men in uniform:

> It was not just the Russians. The behaviour of some of [our] troops was nothing to brag about, particularly after they came across cases of cognac and barrels of wine. I am mentioning this because there is a tendency among the naive or malicious to think that only the Russians loot and rape.

Nevertheless, the armies of the Western Allies committed nothing on the scale of the Russian assault on the women of Berlin and East Prussia. The war in the West had been fought in a different atmosphere, generally adhering to different rules and expectations. Neither Britain nor America had suffered the humiliating and horrific consequences of defeat and Nazi occupation. Allied troops were certainly conquerors but they were also to some degree liberators.

But ultimately the reason for the better behaviour of the Western troops was probably not political or moral but economic. Western troops were better supplied with the two currencies that mattered in Year Zero Germany, cigarettes and food, so they did not need to rape. As Bill Deedes, major in the King's 12th Royal Rifle Corps and later an outstanding journalist, remembered: 'The Germans were very hungry. The girls would get at my riflemen for a tin of sardines.'

'Justified revenge'

Alcohol played a huge part in fuelling the Rape of Berlin. There are many anecdotes from early summer 1945 that indicate that Soviet troops often behaved quite well to civilians until they found the booze. However, the rapid advance of the Red Army from the Oder to the suburbs of the city had given little time for stocks in homes, shops, cafés and restaurants to dwindle. On 23 April, Hotel Adlon opened its famous cellars to its guests and invited them to drink as they pleased, rather than leave its bottled treasures to the oncoming Reds. Despite their efforts, a large quantity of rare and expensive wine was still there when the Soviets arrived. The vast cellars of the Reich Chancellery were also largely untouched. The discovery of these and other caches of intoxicating drink clearly emboldened many a young Soviet soldier. However, the almost medieval sack of the city had deeper and more premeditated origins.

For four years Russian propaganda had driven home the message that this was a war for survival: a war that the Soviet Union had not started or wanted – a war against a merciless ideological and racial foe that was bent upon enslaving and exterminating the Slavic peoples.

Millions of innocent Russians had been murdered by the fascist invader and German behaviour in Russia between 1941 and 1944 was rightly compared to that of the Mongol hordes in the 13th century.

All Soviet commanders understandably used the imagery of justified revenge in their speeches and bulletins, especially generals Zhukov and Konev who led the assault on Berlin. They agreed with Stalin that the German people were now about to receive their just desserts for the appalling atrocities that their troops had inflicted upon the Russians throughout almost four years of war.

Eisenhower, the Western Allied commander-in-chief, agreed: 'The Germans are being repaid in the same coin.'

Kill a German

The Soviet military newspaper *Krasnaya Zvezda* (Red Star) hammered home the message to its uniformed readers: 'Berlin has not yet paid for the sufferings of Leningrad.' The popular Soviet writer and journalist Ilya Ehrenburg spelt it out for the men and women in the Soviet ranks in his chilling 1942 article 'KILL': 'If you have not killed at least one German a day, you have wasted that day. If you kill a German, kill another.' And Ehrenburg gave Red Army men explicit instructions on how to behave when visiting Berlin: 'Kill a German and jump on his woman.' As ever throughout history, rape was the ultimate weapon to demoralize and humiliate a beaten enemy and emphasize their total defeat and impotence.

Not all were rapists

Not all Soviet troops were rapists. Many older men in the Soviet ranks were uneasy about the actions of their younger, drunken comrades, feeling that their behaviour besmirched the name and noble cause of the Red Army. Local commanders knew the regulations against looting and rape but often also realized that it was almost impossible to rein in their war-hardened men. In time, numerous Soviet veterans would express their shame at the events of April–May 1945 but would then admit that they just had to go along with their comrades: taking part in the mass rapes was an act of bonding and celebration at having survived until what was hopefully the end of their war.

Tactical error

Some thoughtful Soviet commanders and strategists appreciated that the violent rape of Berlin and East Prussia was seriously unhelpful to Soviet post-war ambitions. It confirmed all the worst Nazi propaganda stereotypes of the Slavic peoples as Asiatic barbarians. Russia's troops had acted exactly as Goebbels had predicted.

The violence against German civilians was also a tactical error. It only encouraged the last battalions of the Wehrmacht to fight as long as they could, in order to win time for more of their compatriots to surrender to the less vengeful armies in the West. And once peace had been agreed, the rulers of the new Soviet Occupied Zone and later the German Democratic Republic found that the events in Berlin at the end of the war cast a long shadow that alienated much of their population.

Acts of kindness

There were, of course, many instances of Soviet men acting in a restrained and civil manner to those under their sway. Berliners witnessed many acts of kindness to the very young and the very old. One incident in particular deserves to be remembered for the light it sheds on the feelings of many Russian soldiers in those days.

A Red Army commissar confronted a number of Scandinavian citizens in the Swedish Embassy, knowing that some of them had almost certainly been volunteers in the Nordland Division of the SS and most of them had been sympathetic to the Nazi cause – until Stalingrad, of course. The commissar held a young Danish boy at gunpoint, the son of a staff member of the Danish Legation, and threatened to kill him. But first he described the treatment his family had received from the Germans when they invaded his home town.

His parents had been murdered and his neighbours' womenfolk had been raped and killed. He and his family were Jewish, and so he understood what had happened to his wife and his children when they were taken away by the SS, yet he found the humanity to calm himself and put his revolver back under his uniform.

As the terrified Scandinavians looked on, he let the boy go: 'I won't shoot him but you must admit, I would have reason enough. So many people are crying out for revenge.'

Treacherous fanatics

Some Soviet commanders tried to maintain the traditional military code of conduct that governed the treatment of civilians. On 30 April a Soviet brigade surrounded the town of Demmin, north of Berlin in Western Pomerania. Like many Soviet units in that area, its commander had instructions to drive as far west as possible and seize territory for the USSR before the British arrived. He offered the town's leaders the chance to surrender quickly and quietly and he promised to respect the townsfolk as long as there was no resistance from them.

These discussions were interrupted by an outbreak of gunfire by SS and Hitler Youth fanatics, which killed three Soviet negotiators. The Nazi loyalists also blew up the town's bridges as an act of defiance. In response, the commander had little choice but to flatten and raze the town. As a result of this descent into conflict, the town was burned to the ground: there were around a thousand civilian casualties, a number of rapes and the suicides of entire terrified families, who could not face the rage of attackers who had lost a number of their comrades to treachery.

Most Soviet commanders would not have given the good people of Demmin the chance of a peaceful surrender. They reckoned three days of sack and pillage was the reward their men deserved.

Germans refuse to surrender

Throughout April 1945, many front-line Russian troops were exasperated and infuriated by the pointless refusal of the German armed forces to surrender. German tenacity in the face of certain defeat embittered those Russian troops who needlessly lost many comrades in the final days of street-fighting in the rubble of Berlin. Joseph Stalin, the ruthless Russian dictator, understood what his men had been through and what they were thinking. When a leading Yugoslav partisan complained about atrocities committed by Russian troops in the Balkans, he refused to punish the offenders:

> Imagine a man who has fought from Stalingrad to Belgrade across thousands of kilometres of his own devastated land, across the bodies of his dead comrades and his loved ones. How can such a man react in a normal way? And what is so awful in his trifling with a woman after such horrors?

Similarly, Stalin appreciated that his victorious warriors in Berlin deserved a few days' 'rest and recreation'. The depth of the Soviet need for revenge was well captured by the US journalist Virginia Irwin, while conversing with a senior officer in the Russian Guards on 28 April. She asked the Soviet commander if Berlin was his greatest battle. He replied in French that it was not: 'To us there were greater battles. In those, we lost our wives and children.' And, he continued, every man that he had selected for his staff had also lost his entire family in the Great Patriotic War against Hitler.

Chapter 5
Fading Hopes, 30 April, 6 a.m.

Battle for the Reichstag

At dawn on 30 April, the men of the 150th 'Idritskaya' Rifle Division began their assault on the Reichstag. Soviet intelligence suggested that the defenders were numerous, possibly several thousand in number, but the real figure turned out to be nearer 5,000. They were thought to be an ill-equipped and motley assortment of SS and Wehrmacht troops, padded out with *Volkssturm* and Hitler Youth volunteers, and were not expected to be particularly well supplied or well organized.

In fact, the defenders had just been stiffened by a cohort of more than 250 useful men from the *Kriegsmarine*, who had been carried into Berlin by air several days before on the orders of Admiral Dönitz. There were also some men of the SS Wiking Division among them, passionate Nazis from across Europe who had an ideological interest in fighting the Red Army.

Two obstacles lay before the Russian troops. The wide grassy square of Königsplatz in front of the Reichstag, which had been transformed into a deeply cratered landscape that resembled the battlefields of the First World War, and beyond that a number of hastily dug ditches. Russian shelling had encouraged water from the nearby river Spree to seep into these ditches, providing Germany's former parliament with its own moat. The great building itself was still standing but the battering it had taken had created a murderous battleground inside its walls that favoured the hidden defender more than the visible intruder.

The first companies of the 150th to advance that morning had not gone far, 50 metres or less, when they were caught in crippling crossfire. They had not realized that German troops also occupied the Kroll Opera House on the other side of the square. Thirty minutes later, a detachment of Soviet riflemen was sent to the street at the rear of the opera house but they failed in their task of winkling out the Germans inside. By 10 a.m. most of the men in the first Russian wave had been picked off by German snipers firing from the upper floors of the Reichstag, who had the advantage of height and an unimpeded view of their targets below.

Tanks sent to provide support for the 150th were themselves falling prey to the anti-aircraft artillery in the impregnable concrete gun tower at the Tiergarten. After massive losses, the Russians finally arrived at the edge of the moat at around 6 p.m., almost 12 hours after the assault began. There was another hour of carnage before they finally reached the heavily defended doors of the parliament building, where they met with a hellish mixture of disciplined rifle fire, grenades and *Panzerfaust* rockets.

When successive companies of the 150th reached the Reichstag entrance, they found a wall of Russian dead blocking their way, while the defenders were now ensconced in a number of prepared positions on the floor above them and were hurling down a hail of grenades.

Sacrificed for propaganda

Although the battle for the Reichstag was a microcosm of the wider Battle for Berlin, the action that day was futile and pointless. The building had no strategic significance and little symbolic value either, particularly for the Germans. They fought because defence and the delay of inevitable defeat were the only tactical options available to them. The Soviets, however, desperately wanted to capture the magnificent but empty hulk of a building that they believed to be the very symbol of their enemy's capital city. Stalin had demanded that it be taken in time for him to announce its capture at the May Day parade in Red Square.

That day the commander of the 150th, the fearful Major General Vasily Shatilov, squandered the lives of hundreds of his men trying and failing to appease the dictator back in Moscow. Soviet commanders in Berlin even sent a congratulatory message to Stalin announcing that the Red Flag was now fluttering above the Reichstag, while their men had yet to reach the moat and were being gunned down in droves.

In order to achieve the propaganda effect required back home in Mother Russia, the Soviet Air Force dropped several large red banners on to the Reichstag roof, hoping that they would catch on its statuary. A red flag was then briefly hoisted by a Kyrgystani Soviet soldier on the night of 30 April but as his heroic exploit took place in the dark, no photograph could be taken. The flag was removed before first light by the defenders and the final iconic image required by Stalin was only taken once the building had been cleared on 2 May.

Red Army soldiers raise the Soviet flag over the Reichstag, but the actual fighting had taken place the previous night and this was merely a publicity shot ordered by Joseph Stalin.

A hollow victory

For most Berliners, the Reichstag was nothing more than the abandoned talking-shop of the weak democratic republic that Hitler had swept away in January 1933. For 12 years it had mostly lain empty, though it was used at times as a storage area for government stationery and office furniture. Hitler disliked the gloomy Prussian relic and preferred to hold key Nazi Party gatherings at the nearby Kroll Opera House. He believed that its dramatic architecture and sharp acoustics offered a finer stage for his set-piece speeches.

If the battle for the Reichstag had any historical significance, it was that through sheer will and force of numbers it was eventually taken by the Red Army, if a day too late for Stalin's liking. The Russians successfully captured their objective because the tanks that supported their infantry that day had fuel, but the three German Panzers that were stationed nearby on Museum Island did not.

The German defenders perished trying to save something that meant nothing to their leaders and the Russian attackers died because Stalin wanted to add a little extra to his speech on International Workers' Day. Nevertheless, Allied morale was cheered by the taking of the Reichstag. For Nazi Germany, it signalled the extinguishing of hopes that had been fading since the summer of 1943.

Fading German hopes

The loss of Stalingrad in February 1943 had been a serious defeat. It punctured the sense of invulnerability that had surrounded Hitler and Nazi Germany since the start of the war. The number of casualties that Germany suffered is difficult to calculate with any precision as the battle raged across several related fronts and over a period of more than five months. However, German losses certainly amounted to more than 400,000 men and the other Axis powers involved (Italy, Romania, Hungary and Croatia) lost a similar number in total.

The illusion of strength

Yet despite the catastrophe at Stalingrad, in early summer 1943 it did not seem likely that the Third Reich would collapse so completely in less than 24 months. At worst, Germany seemed to be facing a longer, more defensive war akin to the Eastern war of 1914–18.

An army had been lost at Stalingrad, thanks in large part to Hitler's intransigence, but after three and a half years of war the Wehrmacht still had a record number of men in uniform. The German armed forces were well-trained, well-equipped and battle-hardened by the two years of war in the East and they were for the most part well led with one qualification: Hitler's interference and the reluctance of several key senior officers to confront him and disagree with his policies quickly enough. But despite Stalingrad, morale was generally high at the Front and was still holding up at home.

The German economy also seemed able to supply sufficient materiel without having to go to a total war standing, despite the best efforts of RAF Bomber Command. On the map of Europe, German hegemony still began at the Atlantic and stretched deep into Russian territory. Also, events in Italy were to show that the Wehrmacht could fight a successful defensive war and exact a very high price for any territory that it ceded to the Western Allies.

It was the failure of the massive Panzer offensive at Kursk in July and August 1943 that signalled Germany's inability to win against the vast manpower and industrial power of the Soviet Union, aided by supplies from its Western allies.

Outmanned and outgunned

The illusion that Germany was still a mighty military power was quickly exposed the following year with its failure to defend the Atlantic Wall in Normandy in June and the collapse of Army Group Centre in high summer. By autumn 1944, all of the weaknesses in Germany's position had been cruelly exposed. The Third Reich was outmanned, outgunned and, as in 1914–18, was fighting powerful enemies on several fronts. Not only that but the loss of the oilfields in Romania in August 1944 imposed a strict timescale on the German war effort. Germany could only fight a 20th-century war for as long as its limited stocks of oil lasted.

Ardennes failure

If Germany could no longer hope to win the war, it could try to engineer a split between the Western democracies and Communist Russia. In the opinion of Hitler and his circle of advisers, the Western Allies seemed likely to be more amenable and suggestible to diplomatic overtures than the Russians. Hence the Ardennes Offensive in December 1944, fought for geopolitical as much as for military reasons, was designed to give the Americans and the British a bloody nose in the hope that they would stop and ponder the human cost of pressing on into Germany. Pushing them back to Antwerp and the river Scheldt might convince them that there would be no quick and easy victory in the West. It might also encourage them to undertake a strategic rethink that could be exploited to sunder their compact with Stalin. In the event, German failure in the Ardennes only highlighted the weakness of Germany's position. After initial success, Germany lacked the men, ammunition, planes and fuel to press home any lasting advantage.

Hitler's military blunders

The Ardennes Offensive had largely been Hitler's idea and he had ignored voices in the German High Command who expressed their reservations. The dissenting generals made their calculations in terms of resources because they understood that modern warfare was ultimately about logistics and supply. Hitler, an amateur general at best but an avid reader of the work of Carlyle and Nietzsche, believed that success in warfare depended instead upon will.

He drew the wrong lessons from his blitzkrieg victories between 1939 and 1941. In his view, they had been won because Germany had possessed a national will superior to that of its enemies. His vision of the vast lightning sweep and his determination to enforce it upon weaker peoples had crushed the democracies of western Europe.

In reality, Hitler's defeated foes had been ill-prepared for war in material and psychological terms. Germany had also enjoyed a significant but short-lived superiority in terms of its trained manpower and weaponry. The Ardennes Offensive was an attempt to recreate something of the elan and bravura that had brought such startling success at the start of the war but it was a mistake to add to the others he had made since 1941.

From liberators to oppressors

From the moment German troops advanced into Soviet territory in June 1941, they found that significant numbers of Soviet citizens welcomed them as liberators. This was particularly the case in the border lands around the Russian core of the USSR, where the apparatus of the Communist Party had crushed national identities from the Baltic lands to the Ukraine. However, the peoples of the Soviet Union who had been oppressed by Moscow quickly realized that German oppression under Hitler had a familiar, ruthless tone.

Thanks to National Socialist racial ideology, the potential to harness nationalist support across eastern Europe against the Soviet Union was squandered. It was impossible for Hitler to see the peoples in these territories as worthy allies. It was a huge strategic error. Hitler also made serious tactical mistakes, none more damaging than his decision to split his forces during the advance upon Moscow in 1941 by diverting a significant proportion of his troops towards Kiev. The threat against Moscow was fatally weakened and the chance to 'behead' the Soviet Union was lost forever.

Hitler's distrust of the generals

Believing that war could be won by willpower rather than the things that bothered his generals such as logistics, resources and detailed planning, Hitler soon fell out with the German officer class. In his view, they were not prosecuting the war with sufficient vigour. They were over-educated in the science of war but understood little of the realities of battle that he had mastered in the trenches of France and

Belgium. They were too cautious and always too ready to overestimate the strength and resolve of the enemy.

As the war swung against Germany in 1943, his impatience with his generals soon turned to distrust – yet he was always on the lookout, hoping to find the next great commander who could turn the war back in his favour. He could never understand why his officers wanted to withdraw their men from battle in order to regroup, re-equip and remotivate. To Hitler, this was simply the result of their insufficient will to take the war to the enemy and possibly even evidence of treason.

When his torturers reported back from their dungeons, Hitler was not surprised to learn that many in the German military elite knew about the 20 July assassination plot, even if they had not actually supported it or been involved in it. This simply reinforced his belief that they were not to be trusted, hence his repeated refusal to allow commanders to withdraw or retreat. As a result, an ever-increasing number of German units found themselves encircled by a nimble Red Army that had learned from the Wehrmacht how best to integrate airpower, artillery and infantry to implement successful blitzkrieg.

Fortress Cities

Hitler's next great hope, the policy of creating Fortress Cities to serve as impregnable bulwarks to halt the Red Army advance, was also anathema to the German High Command. It tied down large numbers of men and their equipment in one fixed spot which the Soviets could easily bypass and return to at their leisure, once they had captured the surrounding territory. Two of the Fortress Cities,

Königsberg and Breslau, did hold out well in memorable sieges, forcing the Soviets to devote considerable resources to their subjugation. But the Soviet Union had resources to spare and these two long sieges had no impact on the direction of the war. Once the defenders ran out of munitions, their only option was to surrender and join the long columns of German prisoners heading east.

The Fortress City concept was the very antithesis of the mobile, lightning campaigns that had stunned and terrified the world in the first two years of the war. In later memoirs, numerous German observers also noted that the Wehrmacht had seemed so modern and motorized in 1939 but by 1945 it had often become dependent on horsepower in the traditional sense of the word. It was the Allies, even the Soviets in their lend-lease Studebaker trucks, who travelled at speed in the latter stages of the war.

Wonder weapons distraction

The German war effort was also distracted and hindered by Hitler's hope that his scientists and technologists could design new weapons that would turn out to be game changers. Again, the Germans failed to learn from the Allies. Allied air forces tended to concentrate on a few successful designs such as the Hurricane, the Yakolev 3, the P51 Mustang and the Avro Lancaster and then develop and refine these models in large numbers. The Luftwaffe, on the other hand, wasted time developing a much wider range of specialist planes that were eventually often made in very small numbers and proved to be of limited tactical value.

The Messerschmitt ME 163 Komet exemplified this desperate search for a wonder weapon that could neutralize the enemy's numerical advantages. The Komet was designed to intercept Allied bomber squadrons heading towards German cities and was capable of 700 mph (1,127 kph). However, the number of minutes it could spend in the air before running out of fuel was seriously limited, and it was very dangerous to fly and land. In spite of the fact that over 300 Komets were built, they managed a mere 17 kills against ten losses. The money that was misdirected into projects like the Komet could have re-equipped many squadrons with planes that had a proven combat record such as the Messerschmitt 109, planes that were badly needed by the Luftwaffe in 1944 and 1945.

The V1 and V2 rockets terrified enemy civilian populations, but arrived too late and in insufficient numbers to make any difference to the outcome of the war. Other weapons were not only impractical but were also exorbitantly expensive in terms of research and development: projects like the Schwerer Gustav railway cannon (a lumbering monster that fired only 48 rounds in action at the siege of Sevastopol before its barrel wore out) and the Panzer VIII Maus (a tank so large and heavy that few bridges could bear its weight). They fascinated Hitler but distracted many of Germany's best technicians from developing simpler, cheaper weapons that could have made a difference in the field.

Failure to develop U-boats

Hitler's relative lack of interest in naval matters also cost Germany dearly. He rightly pinned his hopes on the U-boat, realizing that surface craft were of limited value to his war plans. Perhaps he remembered that the Kaiser's U-boat fleet had wrought great havoc on the British and French merchant navies. In December 1916, with shipping losses at an all-time high, Lloyd George's Cabinet had even considered approaching the German government with an offer to discuss a ceasefire.

What Hitler certainly failed to remember, though, was that by 1918 the Allies had contained the U-boat menace. New tactics in the form of escorted convoys, new technologies for spotting submarines and the deployment of fast destroyers equipped with depth charges had minimized the threat from the Kaiser's 'wonder weapon'.

The natural evolutionary response should have been to build a new breed of U-boats that were faster and able to travel longer distances underwater. Germany eventually did decide to develop a new class of super-subs, the Type XXI, but the planning of these sleek, aerodynamic boats only began in 1943.

The Type XXI was the first submarine capable of travelling very long distances fully submerged. Its electro-diesel engines were quiet, making it difficult for an enemy to detect them, and it could quickly recharge its batteries without surfacing, thanks to an effective snorkel system. This was an exceptionally powerful stealth weapon that could have had a serious impact upon the Allied fleets but only four ever entered service with the *Kriegsmarine*. Of these only two undertook a combat patrol very late in the war and they recorded no kills.

None of Hitler's wonder weapons fulfilled their early hopes and in any case the speed of the Third Reich's collapse in 1944 and early 1945 left little time to manufacture and deploy them in significant numbers.

Himmler given command

In desperation, and distrusting his military commanders, Hitler looked instead to men who had proven their worth through their service to the Party. He was keen to transfer control of Germany's armed forces from the old professional elite that had failed him to those who were driven by Nationalist Socialist fervour. Heinrich Himmler seemed a logical choice as he had excelled in the two main aspects of his role as Reichsführer. First he had transformed the SS, originally a small force of several hundred bodyguards, into a dedicated paramilitary and security organization with more than a million carefully selected members. The Waffen SS, infused with a fervent crusading spirit, had already proven its worth in battle. He had also masterminded the complex organizational job of collecting and destroying the Jewish populations of every Nazi-controlled country in Europe.

The People's Storm

In late 1944, Hitler gave 'loyal Heinrich' a new task: to create a popular militia encompassing every German male between the ages of 16 and 60 not yet conscripted into the armed forces. This People's Storm or *Volkssturm* was expected to comprise five million citizens or more, who would defend their homes and communities against the Bolshevik invader. Himmler quickly organized this new force and the *Volkssturm* armband became a common sight in German streets throughout the last months of the war. It lacked adequate training facilities and sufficient weapons, however, and Hitler's hopes that it would galvanize the military spirit of the German people were never quite fulfilled.

But it was not as toothless as many of its detractors claimed. The *Volkssturm* carried out much of the preparatory work in advance of the Battle for Berlin: digging foxholes and constructing stone barriers at every key junction in the city. Once the fighting reached central Berlin, several observers remarked at the ferocity which some of the younger *Volkssturm* warriors as young as 12 brought to their task, knocking out Russian tanks with *Panzerfauste* and grenades as skilfully as their older brethren.

Failed army commander

Hitler certainly felt that Himmler had done a reasonable job, given the limited time and resources available. He was therefore promoted to a serious military post as commander

Members of the newly sworn-in Volkssturm – *the 'people's storm' or 'Home Guard' – carry heavy machine guns and* Panzerfaust *anti-tank rocket launchers, November 1944.*

of Army Group Vistula in late January 1945, charged with protecting Pomerania and Berlin. As Guderian and other senior generals predicted, he was unequal to the task. Although an exceptional bureaucratic planner, he was immediately swamped by the fluidity and unpredictability of the large-scale battlefield.

When he was relieved of his command after seven disastrous weeks, his special command train was found to contain only one telephone, no other signals equipment and very few relevant maps. It did, however, boast a very fine and well-equipped massage room, where Himmler spent most afternoons with his Swedish masseur, the spy Felix Kersten. Himmler provided no real leadership to the men under his command and in reality commanders in the field quickly learned to bypass him and report directly to the High Command in Berlin.

Hitler's shrinking world

By the time Himmler was relieved of his 'command' on 20 March, the world that Hitler controlled had shrunk even further. Throughout early 1945 the scale of the problems facing Hitler and his commanders had changed so dramatically that the Führer was now clutching at ever thinner and shorter straws. The ability to launch a meaningful offensive on any of the Fronts no longer existed. All that could be done now was to shore up lines that were threatened in so many places, using units that were under-strength, under-supplied and in some cases had almost ceased to function. The idea that Germany could win the war simply disappeared from official and everyday language. Hitler and Goebbels seldom spoke of victory now but used phrases that reflected more limited goals such as 'frustrating and delaying the enemy' and 'keeping our heroic struggle going'.

Losing interest

Observers noted that outside of official meetings to discuss the war situation Hitler seemed increasingly listless. It was clear that he was often not listening to others but was lost in other thoughts. Some observers felt that he had just lost interest in a war that had disappointed all his hopes. General Burgdorf noted that on 20 April he had been unwilling to listen to a full report on the situation in Prussia. He had merely tolerated a brief résumé and then returned to his rooms to sleep.

When he did discuss the direction of the war, it was generally to blame others for the way things had turned out; the generals, the Jews, the stupid Americans who were so easily misled and controlled by their own Jews, and always the semi-American Churchill who had spurned the opportunity of an alliance against the Soviet Union and thereby condemned Germany to fight a war upon two fronts yet again. And on occasion he blamed the German people themselves. They had been put to the test in a historic war, a Darwinian struggle with only two possible outcomes: survival or annihilation. The German people had been found wanting in the judgement of history and they must now bear the consequences.

Retreating into history

Hitler increasingly spoke of the past and liked to remember key moments in the history that he had made in the early years of the Party. He also liked to reflect on moments in the past where victory had been snatched from the jaws of disaster, finding great inspiration in the republican Romans who had suffered defeat after defeat at the hands of the Carthaginians but had ultimately won through and created an empire. The Führer liked to tell and retell the story of the Prussian monarch Frederick the Great and his intimates such as Linge and his aide Otto Günsche would often find him in his room, gazing at the portrait of Frederick which accompanied him everywhere.

Frederick had faced a powerful coalition of Austria, France, Russia, Saxony and Sweden. His lands had been invaded, his funds and his armies were exhausted and Russia was preparing a final invasion in the spring of 1762 that looked likely to wipe Prussia from the map. Frederick was contemplating suicide so that his successor would have a fresh opportunity to negotiate with his enemies, but at that lowest point glorious news arrived from St Petersburg. The hostile Russian empress Elizabeth had died at the relatively young age of 52 and her successor, Peter III, was part German by birth, a Germanophile in his tastes and a friend and admirer of Frederick. After Elizabeth's death, the coalition against Prussia quickly dissolved. Hitler used the tale to support his belief that no situation in history was so desperate that it did not contain a seed of possible victory.

He seemed to have been proved right on 12 April when the news broke that President Roosevelt had died of a cerebral haemorrhage at the small spa town of Warm Springs, Georgia. For a brief moment, this seemed to be the historic miracle that Hitler had been expecting all along. Hope flourished again in the bunker but the atmosphere was soon dampened as Harry Truman stepped seamlessly into the White House, determined to bring the war to a finish as quickly and as thoroughly as possible.

Hopes revived and dashed

At other moments, Hitler took great interest in relatively small and local tactical events that could not possibly change the eventual outcome of the war, but offered brief moments of relief and raised the fading hopes of the loyal few who remained in the bunker. The remaining 15 or so bunker inhabitants spent their last days there straining to learn and make sense of the tiniest morsels of information from the battlefields above.

Every positive moment, like an advance by General Wenck towards Potsdam, met with exaggerated elation. Every negative event, such as when Wenck's men were bogged down south of Schwielow Lake, plunged everyone back into despair. Minor diplomatic events mentioned by foreign news agencies were analysed for their deeper meaning. Molotov not attending the United Nations event in San Francisco; Churchill and Stalin disagreeing over the future of Poland; were these portents of the long-awaited split between the Allies?

The fierce General Schörner

The example of General Ferdinand Schörner especially revived Hitler's fading hopes and convinced him in his view that the will to win at all costs was vital. Schörner was a talented, intelligent commander and a committed National Socialist who served the Nazi Reich with distinction. He held high office in both the NSDAP and the Wehrmacht, acting as an influential point of liaison between two organizations that were often suspicious of each other. Schörner was also a brutal and ruthless commander who was feared by his own men as much as by the enemy.

In his diaries, Goebbels tracked Schörner's rise to prominence in the latter stages of the war. He noted Schörner's exemplary emphasis upon the strictest discipline. The general ordered that any soldier found behind the lines without written orders explaining his presence away from the Front was to be court-martialled on the spot. If found guilty, he was to be immediately executed as a deserter. Any men despatched in this way were strung up, bearing a sign that indicated that as a deserter they had failed to do their duty to protect German women and children.

Goebbels admired the logic of Schörner's decree, noting: 'Of course, his methods work. Every man under Schörner's command knows that he might die at the Front. But he also knows that he will definitely die in the rear.' For his loyalty and his attitude, Schörner was elevated to field marshal in early April and then, in Hitler's political testament of 29 April, appointed commander-in-chief of the German Army. This was by then a titular appointment. Any vestige of real power in the Third Reich lay with Admiral Dönitz on the north coast. In any case, Schörner was fully engaged in trying to suppress the Prague Uprising. Elements of his army continued fighting there until 11 May, four days after the general surrender.

By then, Schörner himself had escaped to Austria. When he was arrested by the Americans, he had assumed civilian garb. Just a few days before, he had been happy to execute men for trying that very same ruse.

Army Group Steiner

If Schörner emerged as Hitler's favourite army officer and raised his hopes, Felix Steiner dashed them and convinced Hitler that all of his suspicions about the army officer class were correct. Like Hitler, Steiner was twice awarded the Iron Cross during his service in the First World War. He was also awarded high honours in 1942 for his role as commander of the SS Wiking Division, a force comprising Nazi sympathizers principally from Scandinavia, the Low Countries and the eastern Baltic lands.

In the Weimar period he had risen to the rank of major but had more success in life after 1935, when he joined the NSDAP and later came to the attention of Heinrich Himmler. The promotions and honours that he received in the war suggest that he was a brave and loyal servant of the Third Reich.

In the chaos after the Russian breakthrough at the Seelow Heights, however, Steiner found himself commanding a disparate mixture of remnants of other larger, shattered formations. Many of the men nominally under his command had lost their equipment and their weapons in the shambolic withdrawal westwards. Yet on the map in Hitler's situation room something called Army Group Steiner existed and it was apparently stationed in a perfect location to take part in a combined offensive against Marshal Zhukov's 1st Belorussian Front.

The phantom army

On 21 April, Hitler ordered Steiner to attack Zhukov's northern flank in support of the German Ninth Army, which would push into Zhukov's column from the south. On paper

Steiner had more than three divisions at his command but in reality there were only two battalions available. They were depleted and many of the men had no combat weapons, so he was in no position to participate in the planned initiative. Steiner offered these facts to his superior officer and they were relayed to Hitler at the situation conference the following afternoon.

The news of Steiner's reasonable refusal to obey the order to attack triggered the last furious outburst of Hitler's anger at the officer class that had betrayed him. Steiner was a traitor and a coward. Instead of fighting to defend Berlin, Hitler believed he was clearly manoeuvring his force westwards to surrender to the Americans. It was men like him that had betrayed National Socialist Germany. Even the SS had gone behind his back and deceived him.

For the first time, Hitler publicly voiced his belief that the war was lost. Everyone else in the bunker was free to go, he declared, but he was going to stay to the end and die in Berlin: 'As I am too infirm to wield a gun in battle, I shall take my own life, as is fitting for the commander of a fortress.'

Chapter 6
Death of a Warmonger, 30 April, 3.25 p.m.

At around 3.25 in the afternoon of 30 April, Hitler finished saying farewell to the remaining staff who had gathered in the central hallway of the bunker. Then he turned and entered the small room that he had been using as an office and a sitting room. After saying some words of goodbye to Magda Goebbels, Eva joined him there. Their final moment of privacy together was briefly postponed because Magda was desperate to speak to the Führer again and try one last time to persuade him to escape to Bavaria.

After Hitler had yet again explained his determination to die in Berlin to the disappointed Frau Goebbels, he and Eva returned to the room and Linge closed the heavy iron security door behind them. The small group of distraught staff and henchmen then began to drift away in search of a seat and a drink, the silence in the corridor only marred by the incessant drumming of the diesel generator. Witnessing Hitler and Eva prepare to go to their deaths had brought home to the other bunkerites their own dire situation.

The room was dim and sparsely furnished and like all the rooms in the Führerbunker it had a low roof. The main feature was a blue and white two-seater sofa, which was accompanied by three matching armchairs, two side tables and two small stools. By the door was a wooden desk. On the walls there were two small Dutch paintings taken from Hitler's apartment in the Reich Chancellery, a still life and a landscape. In addition to these, Hitler's talisman, the portrait of Frederick the Great by Anton Graff, hung above the desk.

The hard stone and concrete floor was softened by a patterned carpet. In the adjoining bedroom there were only two personal items: a framed photograph of his mother Klara and one of his first chauffeur and comrade from the earliest days of the NSDAP, Emil Maurice. The only sign of modernity in Hitler's 'suite' was a radio.

Retrieving the bodies

Hitler's personal adjutant Otto Günsche stood guard outside the room in the corridor and was then joined by Linge, who had been upstairs fortifying himself for the unwelcome task ahead with a glass of schnapps. After a little more than ten minutes, Linge detected the faint smell of gas discharged from a firearm. The ventilation system in the bunker first drew fresh air into the private rooms and then expelled it out into the public spaces and so the two men knew where the whiff of powder smoke had come from.

Günsche said that he heard a shot but Linge later said that he heard nothing. In the *Vorbunker* above, nine-year-old Helmuth Goebbels shouted 'Bullseye', possibly hearing Hitler's pistol or maybe just a mortar landing in the garden.

After respectfully waiting a few more minutes, Linge and Günsche decided that it was time to open the door. Linge called on Bormann: 'Herr Reichsleiter, it has happened.' The three men then entered the room but in the tenseness of the moment Linge and Günsche spotted and remembered quite different details of the scene that they now witnessed. Almost instantly four others were standing in the doorway of the room: Goebbels, Krebs, Burgdorf and Axmann of the Hitler Youth but of these only Axmann lived to tell his tale. His memory confirmed much of Linge's later testimony.

Bullet to the temple

Hitler and Eva were sitting together on the small, narrow sofa about a foot or so apart. The ex-Führer was sitting upright, his feet planted firmly on the floor and his head leaning slightly forward. His eyes were wide open and he was still wearing his standard bunker uniform of a dark grey military jacket, black trousers, black silk socks and black shoes. He had also put on black gloves, perhaps to ensure a firmer grip on the weapon he had been about to use. A thin trail of blood was making its way down from a small bullet hole in his right temple to the middle of his right cheek. His right arm had fallen downwards and was resting limply between the armrest of the sofa and his right thigh. The armrest had stopped him from falling over to his right and on to the floor.

There was a small, thin puddle of blood about the size of a plate on the ground beyond the sofa armrest. Two Walther pistols lay by Hitler's feet and Günsche and Linge recognized them as both belonging to the Führer. The 7.65 mm Walther PPK was empty but the 6.35 mm gun, a spare pistol that he had prepared in case he made a hash of things, was still loaded.

Dressed for lunch

On his left, Eva was wearing the outfit she had put on for her last lunch, a dark dress with white roses and dark stockings. She had taken off her shoes and placed them together neatly on the floor before drawing up her legs, which pointed away from Hitler, on to the sofa. Her upper body and her head were upright, her eyes were also wide open and her lips were closed and pursed. Although her face showed a little sign of strain, it was unharmed and there were no apparent injuries or traces of blood.

All went as planned

There were two distinct odours in the room: the smell of powder smoke from the pistol and, nearer to Eva's body, the strong smell of burnt almonds characteristic of prussic acid. Dr Stumpfegger quickly confirmed the deaths. Both Hitler and Eva seemed to have died as instantaneously and as painlessly as they had hoped. After several weeks of thinking about and discussing how they would despatch themselves, Adolf and Eva had carried out their suicides exactly as they had planned.

Suicide better than capture

Hitler had reiterated his intention to commit suicide, and take his new bride with him, in the final paragraph of the private will that he dictated to Traudl Junge early on 29 April. He had long since decided that death was preferable to being overthrown or having to surrender and he indicated that both bodies should be cremated immediately in the heart of the Chancellery complex: 'the spot where I have carried out the greatest part of my work in the course of twelve years of service to my people'. On a less noble note, he was also concerned that his body might end up as a trophy in a Soviet freak show, like the mummified and waxen remains of Lenin in Red Square.

He had also referred to his suicide plans in his political testament. When the Citadel could no longer be defended, he said, he would take his life himself. In conversations with the bunker staff, he had earlier explained his decision to stay in Berlin to the very bitter end in terms of his duty: he expected every one of his commanders to die at their posts and he could therefore do nothing less.

He ignored every effort by Bormann and Goebbels to engage him in a discussion about carrying on the war from the Alpine Redoubt, the fortifications that had been built around the Obersalzberg. That would be retreat. And there was a secondary motive for his decision to stay and die in the Führerbunker: fear of capture by the Russians.

Several times before he had expressed his worry that he might fall into Russian hands and then be paraded through the streets of Germany and Russia in a cage, as Moscow propagandists such as Ehrenburg had suggested. He had no intention of being captured by an enemy 'who wants to create a spectacle, organized by the Jews, to entertain the masses'. He said as much to Albert Speer when Speer had offered to fly into Berlin on a rescue mission to transport him and Eva to Hamburg in a pair of Fieseler Storch light aircraft. Artur Axmann's equally ridiculous plan to smuggle him out of the burning ruins of Berlin and through the encircling Red Army lines protected by only a detachment of 200 Hitler Youth volunteers had little appeal for the Führer either.

Inspired by Wagner

Hitler had never pursued a normal political career. Instead, his oratorical skills had propelled him into public life following a meeting of the German Workers' Party in 1919.

However, his passionate interest in politics had apparently sparked into life much earlier, thanks to a chance visit to an opera house in his youth. In 1906, the young Hitler had been transfixed by a performance of Wagner's early opera *Rienzi*. On his 50th birthday in 1939, Hitler recalled the impact of that distant evening with his old boyhood friend August Kubizek and mused: 'At that hour it all began.' Hitler loved the music of *Rienzi*, particularly its thrilling militaristic overture, and he demanded that it always be played at the beginning of his vast Party rallies, as he walked through the massed ranks of his supporters en route to his floodlit podium. His most prized possession was the *Rienzi* manuscript gifted to him by Winifred Wagner.

But it was not only Wagner's stirring music that fascinated him but also the political tale that it told. Cola di Rienzo was a man of humble origins in 14th-century Italy, who rose to power by taking on the weak political establishment of his day in order to restore law and order in medieval Rome. Putting down the lawless bandit clans that terrorized the city, he was acclaimed as Tribune of the People.

Rienzo dreamed of creating a new Roman Empire but after some initial military victories he was betrayed by those around him, who failed to live up to the demands of his historic mission. Trusting in the Roman people, he was disappointed when they turned against him. Surrounded by his enemies, Rienzo died at the heart of the city as the ancient Roman Capitol burst into flames around him.

The story entranced the young Hitler and in later life he drew parallels between Rienzo and his own political career. Chatting in 1934 with Robert Ley, the head of the Nazi Labour Front, he explained the influence that the opera had had on his thinking:

> An inn-keeper's son persuaded the Roman people to drive out the corrupt Senate by reminding them of the magnificent Roman empire of the past. I had the vision that I too must someday succeed in uniting the German empire and making it great once more.

So many features of Rienzo's life seemed to mirror Hitler's political and military career that it became a central part of his personal mythology. Now the coming end of his political career reminded him of Rienzi's downfall. He would therefore exit life in a fittingly dramatic manner by being cremated.

Hitler had apparently chosen to finish things in a way that he thought was worthy of his Wagnerian hero. But the operatic Rienzi dies engulfed in flames atop the burning citadel in the heart of Rome, defiantly resisting his foes and shaking his fist at the fickle Roman mob. Hitler's death lacked any such glory. It would be by his own hand in a squalid concrete bunker, hidden away and unseen by the world, deep beneath the ruins of his former capital city.

Cremation plans

Throughout 29 April, Hitler set about preparing for his death. In their memoirs, Linge and Günsche both indicated that Hitler had asked them to procure enough fuel to cremate himself and Eva. They had both been told to put two large blankets in his room, not for warmth but for carrying the bodies up to the Reich Chancellery garden. Linge remembered the shock of receiving Hitler's blunt order to cremate the bodies thoroughly. He only just managed to stutter out the expected reply: '*Jawohl, mein Führer.*'

Günsche and Linge were probably both correct in their differing recollections of the orders they received that afternoon. Knowing that fuel was scarce in the vicinity of the bunker, Hitler had doubtless thought it best to set both men to the task of securing enough petrol to do the job properly. As he said to the secretaries at lunch that day, he was leaving orders for the disposal of his body in a way that no one would ever find it. He wanted nothing but ashes to be left behind. No relics. No exhibits in a museum or a waxwork display in Moscow.

Sourcing petrol

Linge phoned Erich Kempka in the underground car park and asked him to try and source 200 litres of petrol and then take the canisters to the entrance to the Führerbunker as quickly as possible. He explained why so much was needed and swore Kempka to silence. After getting his excuses in first, because the chance of scraping up that quantity of fuel was highly unlikely, Kempka set about seeing what he had in reserve. He would also siphon off what fuel remained in the 60 or so cars that had been damaged when part of the garage roof was bombed on 24 April. Günsche remembered that it was he who had been given the order to source the petrol and that it was his idea to drain the damaged vehicles.

Given the immensity of what Hitler had ordered to be done, the atmosphere in the bunker at that point and the amount of schnapps drunk by many of the dramatis personae that day, establishing what actually happened is difficult. Nevertheless, enough petrol for two cremations was located, thanks especially to Kempka, who remembered that there was an emergency supply hidden underground in the nearby Tiergarten.

Poison capsules

Although he had decided to shoot himself, Hitler began to consider the effectiveness of the poison capsules that were in his possession. He had the foresight to imagine that in the event he might fumble the pistol business through nerves, so it might be best to keep a reserve capsule on the tip of his tongue. And in any case, Eva was committed to taking prussic acid and he therefore needed to check all possibilities on her behalf. There was an astonishing amount of poison in the bunker by the end. Some of it had been supplied by the Reich Security Service, which had commissioned the manufacture of between 3,000 and 4,000 capsules some months earlier for distribution throughout the upper ranks of the Nazi establishment. Dr Morell and a colleague, Dr Stumpfegger, had both thoughtfully left a smaller supply for the use of the bunker staff.

Dog lover

But the capsules in Hitler's study had been gifted by Himmler, now revealed as a traitor and shorn of all the trust that Hitler had once placed in him. Himmler had assured him that the pills were of high quality, but now Hitler needed to make sure, so his beloved Blondi was about to lay down her life in a bizarre experiment. At difficult times in his life, Hitler had found companionship in a pet dog. In the 1914–18 trenches of the Western Front, he had rescued a white fox terrier that had strayed across no man's land from the British lines in pursuit of a rat. Veterans of his regiment later remembered Hitler as the soldier with the funny dog called Fuchsl, which he trained to walk on its hind legs and do tricks.

A succession of German shepherds followed in the 1920s and 1930s. It was a breed that suited his vision of himself as an Aryan warlord and he was impressed by their obedience and loyalty. The last of these was Blondi, bought in the summer of 1942. During spring 1945, she was a beloved fixture of life in the bunker and in his last months Hitler spent hours with Blondi and her litter of five pups, especially the star turn Wulf, who was adopted by Eva and all of the secretaries.

Dogs poisoned

At 3 p.m. on 29 April, Hitler's dog handler, Sergeant Fritz Tornow, held Blondi's jaws open as Dr Haase placed a capsule of prussic acid in her mouth and crushed it with pliers. Instantly it was clear that the poison in Himmler's capsules was lethal. Hitler, Sergeant Tornow and others in the bunker were saddened by Blondi's death, but Hitler consoled himself with the thought that he had already ordered her destruction lest she fall into Russian hands. Tornow immediately buried her in the garden and the five pups followed their mother to the grave the following day, along with Eva's pair of Scottish terriers, Negus and Stasi.

The Soviet counter-intelligence organ SMERSH later searched the garden for the remains of the dogs, then exhumed and examined them. Their bones had become evidence in Stalin's obsessive quest to determine whether Hitler was truly dead or if he had been spirited away elsewhere. Did the well-known dog lover really leave his pets behind or was their killing part of a deception to cover his tracks?

Death of Mussolini

Although his mind was already made up, the news that came in from Italy at around 10 p.m. on 29 April convinced Hitler that he had made the right decision to end matters himself. Two days earlier, Mussolini, his mistress Clara Petacci and several Fascist Party officials had been captured by partisans at Dongo, a village on the western shore of Lake Como, close to the Swiss border. They were shot the following afternoon. Early on the 29th, their corpses were symbolically dumped from a truck at the Piazzale Loreto in Milan, where 15 civilians had been murdered by Fascist agents the previous autumn. The bodies were violently abused by an angry crowd, who shot and beat them before they were strung up from the roof of a nearby petrol station. Kicked repeatedly and smashed by hammers, Mussolini's face was soon an unrecognizable pulp.

An observer in the bunker watched Hitler read the transcript of the radio signal and underline three words in pencil: 'hanging upside down'. At around 1.30 a.m. he called a group of his bodyguards together and informed them of his decision to commit suicide later that day. He shook the hand of every man in the group and released them from their oath of loyalty to him, encouraging them to try and reach the Western Allies.

The Red Army approaches

Early on the morning of 30 April, Hitler told Linge to follow him to the telephone exchange, where a line to General Weidling had been restored. He signalled to him to take care so as not to wake the bunkerites scattered around the corridor, trying to catch some sleep on the sofas or on camp beds. Bottles of schnapps and loaded pistols littered the floor.

A message to Weidling was sent and from the reply Hitler learned again what he already knew: the city could not be held, the Russian line could not be pierced, there was no possibility of relief. Despite ferocious resistance, the Red Army was inching ever deeper into the Citadel but losing huge numbers of men as it tried to bludgeon its way into the Reichstag building. Despite this sliver of good news, the situation across Berlin was bleak. Oblivious to Linge and the signal officer, Hitler stood still and muttered quietly to himself: 'That is no longer an option, here I stay.'

At around four in the morning, Hitler had a brief final conversation with Dr Haase to discuss how to ensure that he died at the same time as Eva. The wisest strategy, they agreed, was to load two pistols in case one jammed and to prepare two capsules each in case one was a fake or a dud. Turning to Eva, who feared she might lose her resolve, Haase counselled her to bite down hard the moment she heard the shot from Hitler's pistol.

Three hours later, at dawn, Eva went up the concrete steps that led out to the badly shattered Reich Chancellery garden. Despite the risk of bursting shells, she stayed there for a few moments, hoping to catch a glimpse of the sun, but the sky was heavy and darkened by the pall of smoke that hung over central Berlin. There was also nothing but gloom at Hitler's final military situation meeting at midday. The reports revealed nothing new, merely the tedious litany of dwindling ammunition, the impossibility of bringing in supplies by air, fading morale and the ever-closer Russians. Weidling was convinced that the battle for the city would end that evening and Wilhelm Mohnke, the commander of the forces around the Citadel, agreed. Hitler understood.

Final lunch

Eva dressed for lunch in a black dress with a collar of white roses, one that Adolf had often said suited her particularly well. She gave some gifts to her maid Liesl and presented Traudl with a silver fox fur coat. In the event, Eva couldn't face lunch and stayed in her room, while Hitler chatted to the secretaries over his final meal of spaghetti with a cabbage and raisin vinaigrette salad. He sat with Traudl, Gerda and the Chancellery cook Constanze Manziarly and spoke about his place in history. The post-war world would denigrate him and the German people would face very difficult times in defeat, but he was confident that in times to come later histories would treat him more fairly. The two hours after lunch were taken up with thanks and farewells.

At 2.45 p.m., Günsche called together the remaining inhabitants on both levels of the Führerbunker. Hitler was subdued and those that he spoke with, such as Traudl Junge, could make little of the words that he muttered to them. In several cases, Eva, smiling but nervous, spoke for him, hugging Traudl and urging her to do her best to get out: 'It may still be possible. Give my love to Bavaria.' After thanking Linge for everything he had done for the Führer over the years, she had a special message for him: 'If you meet Gretl, say nothing about how Fegelein met his death.'

Goebbels again urged Hitler to flee to Obersalzberg but he shook his head and ordered that any aircraft waiting for him and his entourage should be used to ferry women and children out of the city. Taking Hitler's hand, Goebbels assured him that he would stay to the end and follow his example. Magda again pleaded with Hitler to save himself, only to be disappointed.

Once the group had begun to disperse, Hitler reminded Linge of his instructions, stressing the importance of burning his corpse thoroughly and destroying all of the personal possessions in his rooms. He also ordered him to attach himself to one of the groups planning to break out from the Citadel and head west. When Linge wondered if there was any point in carrying on, Hitler answered him: 'Do it for the Man of the Future.' They shook hands and took a small step towards each other, then each man raised his arm in the Hitler salute.

Dicing with death

Those who watched the iron door of their temporary tomb slowly close behind them had no doubt that Hitler and Eva would carry out their dreadful decision. Hitler had already made it clear that he was terrified of being captured and subsequently humiliated and punished by the Allies, so he would not change his mind. Also, he had faced death before on a few occasions.

He faced less danger in the 1914–18 war than previously thought and probably less than he later claimed in his speeches and in conversations with old foes and comrades. Recent research has suggested that Hitler spent much of his time as a courier taking messages from the Front to HQ, a much safer job than that of a company runner who would have carried messages between points under direct fire. Nevertheless, he did see action in the trenches as his injuries and final gassing in 1918 indicate and his army record reveals that he was a competent, conscientious soldier throughout the war.

In the 1939–45 war he knew the value of being seen to share the burdens of the ordinary soldier. Even in the latter days of the war, his arrival at the Front electrified 'his men', boosted their morale and convinced them that they were risking their lives for a truly worthy commander. During the Polish campaign in 1939, he visited units in forest areas where enemy snipers were known to be operating. With little attempt at disguise, he openly chatted with the lower-ranking troops about their experience of the war so far and he sat and ate with them in their field kitchens.

And during the campaign to secure the Caucasus and the road to the oilfields of Baku, he flew to Rostov on Don near the Sea of Azov in a small Messerschmitt. Hitler claimed that he had enjoyed the flight immensely and calmly dismissed the very real threat of attack by the Soviet Air Force. Then at a field meeting near the Smolensk Front in 1943, Soviet troops attacked the airfield where Hitler's plane had landed and were closing in on the complex where Hitler was working with senior officers. The officers were concerned for his safety but after giving a few instructions for dealing with the intruders, he returned to the map and the matters in hand.

He was again in the thick of things when he visited the important industrial city of Zaporizhia on the Dnieper in south-eastern Ukraine in the winter of 1942–43. The Wehrmacht officers commanding the city were desperate for Hitler to leave as the important power station there was under attack. However, Hitler preferred instead to remain in the city for four days, involving himself in every aspect of its defence.

Finally, after the 20 July bomb blast, the Reich Security Service had insisted on a thorough examination of all visitors entering the Wolfsschanze compound, but Hitler ensured that decorated men did not have to undergo the indignity of being 'padded down' by the SS guards and could walk straight past them and into his presence.

Hitler therefore exhibited a certain degree of personal bravery during the Second World War, though his exploits were certainly well publicized by Goebbels and often orchestrated to enhance his image as 'the Great Commander'. As for Eva, she had demonstrated her courage, or her blind devotion to Hitler, by returning to Berlin in March. But given the circumstances in which Hitler found himself, it was more a question of suicide being the lesser of two evils. Bravery did not really come into the equation.

Removing the bodies

When the remaining bunkerites learned that Adolf and Eva were dead, a palpable wave of relief spread through both levels of the bunker. The event they had all been waiting for had happened at last. Finally, they were free to start thinking about their own futures. Hitler's aides and guards, however, still had the clearing up to do. The first priority was to dispose of the bodies and start the cremation process as quickly as possible.

At about 3.40 p.m., Hitler's body was lifted from the sofa and laid on a blanket on the floor, which was then folded over the corpse. Linge took the feet and another man whom he did not know took the head. The corpse was then carried along the corridor to the steps that led to the garden. Linge was helped up the steps by several SS officers from Hitler's bodyguard, who seemed to appear on the scene very quickly and out of nowhere. Perhaps the tidy bureaucrat Bormann had thought ahead and arranged some extra help.

Those who saw the corpse being carried out remembered Hitler's lower legs dangling limply below the end of the blanket, revealing his trademark black trousers, black silk socks and black leather shoes. The corpse was hurriedly laid down on some flat sandy ground a couple of metres or so from the bunker door with the feet pointing towards it. There was little sense in going any further into the deeply cratered lunar landscape, which had once been an immaculate garden. Given the continual threat of shelling, the corpse-bearers were keen to stay close to the shelter entrance.

Eva arrived a few seconds later in Günsche's arms. She was laid by Hitler's side, a foot or so away from him. Down in the study she had been attended to by Bormann but as he began to carry her along the corridor Kempka stepped in and took Eva from his arms. He later explained his action: he could not bear to see Eva's body being touched by a man she had despised in life. At the bottom of the steps, the sturdy Günsche took over the grisly relay for the last few steps up and into the garden. As he laid her down at Hitler's right-hand side, he noticed that the trickle of blood from the hole in his temple was now spread across the Führer's face.

Funeral pyre

The funeral was suddenly interrupted by a salvo of explosions, possibly from a Katyusha rocket launcher. Although the two principal corpses were untouched, this round of shelling disturbed many of the other bodies under the garden yet again. They were mostly wounded troops and Berliners who had died in the hospital under the Reich Chancellery. When the cascade of shells or rockets briefly paused, Linge, Kempka and Günsche took turns to dash out from safety and pour out the contents of one of the petrol canisters piled up on the stair landing. A Reich Security Service officer, Hans Hofbeck, helped keep the door open. Between them, Linge, Kempka and Günsche managed to drench the corpses with the contents of eight or nine 20-litre petrol canisters.

Earlier in the day Kempka had doubted whether enough petrol could be found to do a thorough job but now there was more than 300 litres in the bunker. Someone, possibly Bormann, had in the meantime sourced an additional quantity of fuel and placed it in the machine room. It had perhaps come from the supply that had been salvaged from one of Berlin's airports before the Russians arrived.

Goebbels had arrived with matches but getting the pyre to light proved difficult. Renewed shelling and the heavy petrol fumes made it difficult to approach the bodies and the 'undertakers' had to shelter behind the fireproof door. Gusts of wind blew out the matches until either Bormann or Kempka soaked a rag with fuel and threw this burning spill on to the outstretched couple. As the door was quickly drawn almost shut, a huge bright flame crowned with thick black smoke began to rise up above the Citadel.

The witnesses to the physical destruction of the Führer and his wife – Linge, Kempka, Günsche, Goebbels, Bormann, Dr Stumpfegger, General Burgdorf and General Krebs – peered out from the partially open door for a few brief minutes and watched the fire take hold of its prey. Together they shouted 'Heil Hitler!' and offered one final Hitler salute to the burning dead. Once they had seen enough to convince themselves that the fire would hold and destroy all traces of the bodies, they turned and helped each other down the steps. They did not return to the garden.

A future without Hitler

Linge and Günsche now had to re-enter Hitler's rooms and destroy their contents as ordered. With the Russians breathing down their necks, the job had to be done quickly. Documents, uniforms, medicines and all other personal items were speedily disposed of, even the carpet stained with Hitler's blood. The *Rienzi* manuscript disappeared around this time, probably a victim of this breakneck clear-out of potential Hitler memorabilia.

Delaying the news

For Goebbels, Bormann and the other leaders, the next task was to consider whether to broadcast a communiqué to the German people. They decided to delay issuing the news of Hitler's death for as long as possible. It was vital that the German troops in contact with the enemy continued to fight as long as they were able: every hour that passed allowed the columns of refugees to stumble that little bit further west and out of Soviet hands. As a result, the Reichs-Rundfunk-Gesellschaft, the state broadcasting corporation of the Third Reich, would only inform the German people of Hitler's death more than 31 hours after the event, late on 1 May. Hitler had apparently fallen heroically, to the very last leading the men of his command post in the fight against Soviet communism.

Five hours after Hitler died, his cook, Constanze Manziarly, prepared an evening meal for him, perhaps through ignorance of his death or possibly as part of a charade to suppress the rumours that were beginning to be whispered in the tunnels of the Chancellery.

A Russian soldier shows some newly arrived British 'Tommies' the spot where the Russians found the supposed remains of Adolf Hitler and Eva Braun, Berlin 1945.

Ashes to ashes

The job of maintaining the flames until the bones had charred, crumbled and then turned to ash was given to minor characters in the drama: orderlies and guards. SS officers Ewald Lindloff and Hans Reisser supervised the stoking of the fire with petrol. For another three hours or more they continued to pour petrol on to the flames, breaks in the Russian shelling permitting, standing by at the bunker door with spades to shovel away whatever eventually remained. They witnessed the roasting flesh that had been Hitler's face and Eva's leg; the contractions and contortions of the corpses as their soft tissues congealed and then evaporated; the scattering of some of the remains by the persistent Russian shelling; and the shrinking and carbonization of the bones until the gusting wind began to blow away what was left. By 5 p.m. the bodies had burned down into skeletons and by 7.30 little more remained than two small piles of white ash swirling up into the air.

Chapter 7
Aftermath, 1 May, 6 p.m.

The Goebbels' children poisoned

At about six o'clock on the evening of 1 May, the six young children of Joseph and Magda Goebbels were murdered. They were first sedated and then prussic acid was introduced into their mouths, bringing about their rapid, painless deaths. The eldest girl, Helga, had some bruising on her face, which may have resulted from an attempt to struggle against her poisoner(s). As with so many key moments in the final days of the Third Reich, the details of the event were later obscured by different claims and recollections. In one version of the tale, the children were told that they needed to take a special medicine because they were spending so much time down in the dark, unhealthy bunker. Dr Helmut Kunz, a dentist stationed at the Reich Chancellery, certainly later admitted that he had injected the children with morphine.

Once they were asleep, the fatal poison was probably administered by one of Dr Morell's assistants, the SS doctor Ludwig Stumpfegger. Other bunkerites believed that the children were told that they would be travelling to Bavaria the following day and would need a good night's sleep. According to this version, Stumpfegger gave them a sweetened drink containing a sedative and their mother

Magda put the poison in her children's mouths. Another witness thought that their father Joseph had found a doctor in the Chancellery building who was willing to inject a quick-acting poison into his five daughters and his son. In any case, the children were definitely killed because their parents had decided that they had to die.

A 'ray of sunshine'

The Goebbels family had moved into the bunker complex on 22 April, as the artillery of the Red Army could now be heard only too clearly at their idyllic family home on the island of Schwanenwerder on the river Havel, south-west of Berlin. In the dark days of late April, the Goebbels children had been a ray of sunshine in the daily life of the bunkerites. Traudl Junge remembered them as well-behaved, good-humoured and enchanting children who loved fairy tales and funny stories. She enjoyed the time she spent playing games with them up in the *Vorbunker*, even when that was only done to distract them from the sad events unfolding one floor below.

One day they were the star turn of a concert party for the patients in the Reich Chancellery hospital, where they sang their repertoire of German folk songs. They had enjoyed their holiday in subterranean Berlin; playing with Blondi, Wulf and the other pups; being fussed over by the secretaries; getting to eat as many treats as they liked now that their father had relaxed his stern position. Before that, he had decreed that a Party leader's children should eat no more than the standard national rations.

They especially enjoyed teasing the genial Rochus Misch, 'the bunker giant' who manned the radio desk next to the rooms allocated to the Goebbels family. Only the eldest, 12-year-old Helga, was a little distanced from the fun, possibly because she was the most mature or perhaps because she understood more about the serious danger that threatened them all. When their bodies were discovered by the Red Army on 2 May, they were lying together in the bunk beds they had slept in throughout their holiday, in a place they called 'the Cave'. As they were killed just before bedtime, they were wearing their nightclothes and the five girls had their hair tied up with ribbons.

Joseph and Magda's remains discovered

The Soviets had already discovered the remains of their parents. After murdering their children, Joseph and Magda

Joseph Goebbels and his wife Magda with her son from another marriage, Harald Quandt, and their six children: from the left, Helmuth, Helga, Hilde, Holde, Hedda and Heide.

had gone up to the garden at around 8.30 p.m. and done away with themselves. The method of their deaths was also later disputed. They might have taken prussic acid together, or Goebbels may have shot his wife and then turned his pistol on himself. Whatever the method, they were almost certainly both dead by the time Goebbels' adjutant, Günter Schwägermann, stepped out of the stair landing and ordered his SS guard to fire into the two corpses to make sure. That had been Goebbels' last instruction to Schwägermann.

Like Hitler, Goebbels had a morbid fear of being captured alive by the Russians and in common with the deceased Führer he wanted his remains and those of his wife to be burned beyond recognition. But this latter request turned out to be impossible to fulfil. There may have been insufficient time or fuel or men to keep the fires burning as had happened the previous day with Hitler and Eva. As it was, the bodies of Joseph and Magda were only badly charred in places: Joseph had lost an arm to the flames and Magda's face was very badly burned. Both bodies were quite recognizable when they were taken into Soviet custody.

Most important Nazi

With Hitler dead, Goebbels had briefly become the most important Nazi left in Berlin. Hitler had recognized that fact when he promoted him to Reich Chancellor in his last will and testament on 29 April. Göring and Himmler had left Berlin immediately after Hitler's birthday ceremony on the 20th and neither had any intention of returning. As far as Hitler was concerned, they had abandoned him and the Party. Speer, who had certainly regarded himself as a likely successor to Hitler's high office, left the city on the 23rd.

Goebbels, however, was determined to stay by the Führer's side even if that meant disobeying Hitler's continual urging that he send his wife and children away somewhere safer. Others might run but Goebbels would remain loyal to the end and his fanatically Nazi wife supported him to the hilt.

Top of the Russian hit list

There were practical reasons for their decision. He knew that after Hitler he was at the very top of the list of Nazi figures targeted by the Russians. It was almost certain that the organs of Soviet intelligence knew that he was still in Berlin and that their agents were watching out for him. Escaping from Berlin with six small children presented its own difficulties, as did his distinctive appearance and his well-known limp. He knew that he could expect no mercy from the Soviets, for he was always the most ideologically committed National Socialist among the Party leadership elite.

Others carved out careers in the Third Reich because they sought opportunities for power and wealth. Goebbels was a Nazi because he believed in Hitler and his ideas about German racial superiority. Hitler had recognized this in the mid-1920s when he handed him the job of Party leader in the left-leaning city of Berlin, where the Communists were well entrenched. Of all the men at his disposal, Hitler saw that only Goebbels had the energy and intelligence to steer Berlin, barren ground electorally, into the Nazi fold.

Closeness to Hitler

The Führer tolerated sycophantic men like Göring and Himmler as long as they were useful. He saw their weaknesses and used their talents but he never befriended them. With Goebbels it was different. Goebbels had seriously criticized some of Hitler's actions and policies in the early days of the Party and he continued to tell Hitler his mind throughout their 20 years of working closely together.

Hitler appreciated that Goebbels was not a critic because he was hostile or ambitious but because he believed in the NSDAP and its aims and he wanted to ensure its success. Both men admired and liked each other, which allowed them to make cruel jokes at each other's expense at times. Hitler knew that Goebbels was every bit his equal as an orator and was superior in debating and holding the attention of others with his witty conversation. The Führer confided in Linge: 'Goebbels is a giant in a dwarf's body, a man of magnitude.'

Hitler always enjoyed being in the company of the Goebbels family and he made strenuous efforts to successfully reconcile Joseph and Magda when their marriage was threatening to disintegrate in 1938: Goebbels was infatuated with the Czech-Austrian film star Lìda Baarová. Magda had her own private involvements with other leading figures in the Party including one of Hitler's fast-rising favourites, Karl Hanke, who ultimately succeeded Himmler as head of the SS.

Goebbels' closeness to Hitler, however, and his effectiveness as German Propaganda Minister, ensured that he was especially loathed by the enemies of Nazi Germany. In Allied propaganda he was depicted as the poison dwarf, the evil creature by the Führer's side encouraging him in his madness.

A man on a bicycle and a young boy pass by crumpled vehicles and artillery in Oberwallstrasse, central Berlin, which bore the brunt of some of the most vicious fighting, July 1945.

Magda and Hitler

Magda Goebbels had also been the closest to Hitler of all the Party wives. She had campaigned throughout Germany with him before the takeover in 1933 and she was often referred to as 'the First Lady of Nazi Germany'. It was she who organized the replies sent to women from all over Germany and beyond who wrote to the Führer as if he were a matinée idol and she acted as his escort at many of the important public moments in the life of the Third Reich. Her affection for him was genuine and deep.

On the day he died, she begged him on her knees to flee to Bavaria but Hitler simply removed his golden NSDAP pin from his jacket lapel and pinned it on Magda's breast. Given this degree of closeness and friendship with Hitler, Goebbels knew that he and his wife, and possibly their children, could expect a very special level of interrogation and torture in the Soviet prisons that were awaiting them. Following Hitler and Eva's example was, therefore, the logical thing to do.

Ceasefire attempt

On the evening of the 30th, and while Hitler's corpse was still burning, Goebbels and Bormann had tried to engineer a ceasefire with the Soviet Command in Berlin. As evening fell, a cable line between the bunker and the Soviet front line was established. Desperate attempts were then made to contact the enemy command to try and arrange a meeting between General Chuikov and the Russian-speaking Krebs. Goebbels hoped for ceasefire negotiations that might avoid or at least postpone an unconditional surrender. He also asked for safe passage out of Berlin for the remaining inhabitants of the bunker. Eventually, at 4 a.m. on 1 May, Krebs was admitted to Chuikov's headquarters, a suburban house near Tempelhof airfield.

Chuikov was amazed to learn that Hitler was dead and that he had been holed up in a bunker in central Berlin so close to the front-line action since January. Like most senior Russian commanders, he had simply assumed that Hitler would have had the sense to take flight for Bavaria, so that he would inevitably fall into American, rather than Russian, hands. In front of Krebs and his aides, however, he pretended that Soviet Command already knew all about the events in the Citadel. Krebs relayed the key points of Hitler's political testament, which had rearranged the Nazi power structure, and then he handed over the statement from Goebbels requesting a satisfactory conclusion to the war.

The news was relayed to Marshal Zhukov and then on to Moscow, where a sleepy Stalin was resting in preparation for the May Day parade in Red Square. He expressed his disappointment at learning that Hitler had not been captured alive. As regards negotiations, however, Stalin was implacable: only immediate and unconditional surrender by all German forces was acceptable to the Russians.

Suicide or breakout?

Now the bunkerites faced a stark choice: to commit suicide or to attempt a hazardous breakout though the Soviet lines. Goebbels and his wife chose the quick solution. Before ending it all, Magda wrote to her son Harald, the product of her first marriage to the wealthy German industrialist Günther Quandt. Harald was a Luftwaffe officer who had been captured in Italy in 1944 and by the end of the war was in a British POW camp. In her letter, Magda tried to explain the reasons for the horrific actions that she and his stepfather had taken:

> The world which will come after National Socialism is not worth living in ... the children are too good for the world that will come after us and a gracious God will understand me if I myself give them release from it ... be proud of us ... everyone must die and is it not better to live a short, honourable, courageous life than a long life in shameful conditions?

In the early hours of 2 May, generals Krebs and Burgdorf also decided that they could not face the rigours of a Russian prison. After consuming a couple of bottles of brandy thoughtfully provided by SS Brigadeführer Mohnke, they blew their brains out. The diplomat and spy Walther Hewel also took his life that day but preferred to do it with poison.

The fortunes of war

Almost all of the remaining bunkerites made their way to the Reich Chancellery via the crumbling remains of the bomb-damaged link tunnel. There they combined with a number of survivors from the Chancellery, some determined, some terrified, and organized themselves into ten groups of varying sizes, each containing a mix of experienced soldiers and civilians, male and female. The plan as such was to try and go north or north-west and at all costs avoid the southern and eastern districts where the bulk of the Russian forces were concentrated. The streets above ground were dangerous and in the central district they were almost impassable. Fighting was also still going on between the Red Army and scattered remnants of a Panzer brigade that had ended up defending the north-west flank of the Citadel.

The first objective was to try and make it across the few hundred metres between the Chancellery and the railway station near Friedrichstrasse. They hoped it was still in German hands. From there it might be possible to use the underground railway and tram tunnels. It was known that the Soviet military was avoiding using the tunnel network beneath Berlin as they expected that it had been fully wired for explosives.

Now the random luck of war came into play, deciding the fate of each individual who took part in the breakout that day. Very few of the escapees made it out of Berlin and most of Hitler's 'intimates' fell into Soviet hands. Artur Axmann did make it to Lübeck in the British-occupied zone but was arrested in December 1945 and imprisoned for more than three years for organizing a neo-Nazi resistance group. Werner Naumann, a senior official in the propaganda ministry and someone whose company Hitler particularly enjoyed, also made it to the British zone. Like Axmann, he came to the attention of British intelligence as a result of neo-Nazi activities and was arrested in 1953 but released after several months in detention.

Traudl Junge made it out of Berlin and managed to get to the river Elbe, but she was unable to reach the British lines. She was arrested by the Soviets in early July and then spent spells being interrogated in turn by the Russians, the British and the Americans before her final release in Bavaria in 1946. One of the luckier female escapees was Bormann's secretary, Else Krüger, who was captured by the Russians but was then transferred to the British sector for special interrogation. She ended up marrying her British interrogator and lived most of her later life in northern England.

Casualties

Of the Hitler intimates who died in the breakout, Bormann and Stumpfegger probably suffered the most spectacular injuries. Having made it safely to the Friedrichstrasse station, they attempted to cross the river Spree near the Weidendammer Bridge. A Tiger Panzer fortuitously passing in their direction offered them the chance of cover from the hail of Russian bullets that was likely to come their way and the two men clung on to the side of the Tiger until the tank took a hit from a rocket. The explosion 'tossed the men into the air like small dolls'. Although badly shaken and injured, they subsequently made it across the bridge and headed north along the nearby railway tracks.

Making his way in the same direction, Artur Axmann came across two bodies at around 1 a.m. Though he had no torch, there was enough moonlight for Axmann to establish the identity of the corpses. As the Soviets slowly began to clear up the debris of war, the two bodies were eventually buried on 8 May beside the nearest railway station and remained there until discovered by construction workers in 1972. The jaws of both skeletons contained fragments of a glass poison capsule. Forensic investigations strongly suggested that one of the victims was Dr Stumpfegger and DNA tests in 1998 confirmed that the other was Bormann.

Hitler's deputy pilot, Georg Betz, was also badly wounded crossing the Weidendammer Bridge and died a few hours later. And the pretty, buxom cook from the

Chancellery, Constanze Manziarly, must also be presumed dead. Taken away by two Soviet soldiers who wanted 'to check her papers', she was last seen disappearing down a subway tunnel with her captors.

Quickly rounded up

Most of the Chancellery escapees were rounded up quite quickly. Of the bunkerites, Gerda Christian and Otto Günsche had not gone far when they were taken into Soviet custody on 2 May. Given his close involvement in Hitler's death, Günsche was of great interest to Stalin and the NKVD. He was immediately whisked off to Moscow where he remained until 1956. The pilot Hans Baur's attempt to flee came to an end when he sustained serious leg wounds from Russian machine-gun fire.

In these early days of the post-war world, Moscow believed that Hitler had probably been flown out to safety. There was also some speculation that Baur had helped senior Nazi leaders to fly out some of their treasures, including the famed Amber Room that had been stolen from the Empress Catherine's palace at Tsarskoye Selo near St Petersburg.

Like Günsche, therefore, Baur was 'a prisoner of special interest' and came under intense Soviet scrutiny. At one point he considered committing suicide, especially after his leg had to be amputated, but over time his morale rallied and he found the will to survive. He remained in Russian custody until 1955, when the West German Chancellor Konrad Adenauer negotiated the release of most of the remaining German prisoners in the camps and prisons of the Soviet Union.

Wilhelm Mohnke and Dr Ernst Schenck had a surprisingly pleasant introduction to their new life as Soviet prisoners. They were well treated, well fed and very well watered with vodka by the commander of the military unit that had captured them. However, once he reckoned that he had gained as much information as he was likely to get from the two sozzled Germans, they were unceremoniously handed over to the NKVD.

The last bunkerites

The telephone operator Rochus Misch stayed at his post in the bunker after most of the others had left to join the breakout groups. He ventured out into the city just as the Soviets were preparing to enter the bunker area on 2 May and was quickly captured, spending the next eight years in Russian interrogation chambers and labour camps.

Dr Werner Haase was found in the Chancellery hospital on 6 May, still tending to the patients there. It fell to Haase to formally identify the bodies of the Goebbels family. He too was a prisoner of 'special interest' and spent the rest of his life in Butyrka Prison, where he died from tuberculosis in 1950.

There was only one German left in the Führerbunker when the first Soviet troops tentatively descended the concrete steps from the garden. Johannes Hentschel, the electrician who tended the bunker generator and kept the lights on, had decided to take his chances with the Soviets by staying put.

He witnessed the female Red Army officers rummaging in Eva Braun's wardrobe and helping themselves to her black silk and lace underwear.

Not much left: Hitler's command centre in the bunker partially burned out by fleeing SS guards and then further ransacked by Russian intelligence and trophy-hunting troops.

The one who got away

Erich Kempka eluded the Russians longer than most, even though he had been knocked out by the same rocket blast that injured Bormann and Stumpfegger. He later claimed that he had been helped in his escape by a young Yugoslav woman, who gave him civilian clothes and who vouched for him as being her husband when questioned by Soviet troops. Although an unlikely tale, Kempka was certainly in Wittenberg, 70 miles (113 km) south-west of Berlin, by the end of May. By late June he was safely in American hands in Bavaria.

Heinz Linge was initially with Kempka when the breakout began but was much less fortunate, only making it as far as the underground tramway tunnel near Seestrasse in the north-western district of Wedding. Hearing German troops shouting directly above him, Linge climbed out of a shaft that led up on to the street and made himself known to the comrades around him.

Unfortunately for Linge, the troops were German but they were not in Wehrmacht uniforms. He had walked into a unit of German soldiers who belonged to the anti-Nazi National Committee for a Free Germany. Their members frequently served with the Red Army in front-line positions, acting as translators and interrogating prisoners. His life was almost certainly preserved by a friendly Russian sergeant who told him to rip off the SS insignia on his jacket.

Linge remained 'incognito' for several days until he was unintentionally unmasked by Hans Baur at a prison camp near Posen. He was soon on his way to a bug-infested cell in the Lubyanka prison in Moscow, where he was repeatedly tortured by NKVD interrogators desperate to squeeze from him every piece of information about his life alongside Hitler.

Official German surrender

At 6 a.m. on 2 May, General Weidling walked into Chuikov's headquarters and surrendered, then sat down to prepare his final communiqué to the German troops still under his command. He announced Hitler's death by suicide, an act that freed all German soldiers from their oath of loyalty to the Führer. Any further resistance was meaningless and merely prolonged the suffering of Berlin's civilian population and the Wehrmacht's wounded, so all German forces in Berlin were therefore ordered to cease hostilities immediately. Weidling was then taken to Moscow, where he died in 1955.

As news of the order filtered through the city, the guns on the massive flak tower at Tiergarten fell silent and the beleaguered garrison within began to emerge into the daylight. One group of SS men held out near the Spree, but elsewhere in the city the tired and hungry defenders of Berlin gradually emerged from their holes in the rubble and threw down their empty weapons. The war was over and they had survived.

They were alive but their faces and demeanour revealed that they were simply dead men walking, because they had not just lost a war: the world they had fought for was over. They might receive bread and water from the victors, but they knew they would soon be marching eastwards to a new, and probably short, life as a slave.

Under Soviet rule

When the Russian artillery bombardment ended on 2 May, silence enveloped the city. Many Berliners later remembered that moment when they broke into tears as they realized that the bombing and shelling had finally stopped. Now the new masters of Berlin set about establishing order among the ruins. This task was largely in the hands of General Nikolai Berzarin, commander of the 5th Shock Army, the first Soviet unit to enter the territory of Berlin. Berzarin was an intelligent and practical commander who wanted to get the city back to some semblance of normality as quickly as possible. With no radio or newspapers operating in the city, loudspeaker vans toured the streets informing the citizenry that the Battle of Berlin was over.

The bodies of hanged looters and traitors, often young boys who had been conscripted into the *Volkssturm* and had panicked under fire, were taken down from the street lamps and added to the piles of corpses along the main roads of the city. It would take almost six days to complete the task of disposing of those dead that were relatively easy to find. A start was made on sorting out the badly contaminated water supply and restoring the city's gas and electricity infrastructure.

The clean-up begins

Expecting some nocturnal resistance from Nazi fanatics and fearing an outbreak of crime, Barzarin imposed a strict military curfew. Then he set up a civilian police force and appointed an acceptably non-political mayor to establish a new city administration. In each local block, a leader was appointed to organize the clean-up in their locality. Within a couple of days, Red Army personnel were amused to see house-proud German housewives beginning to sweep the dust and debris off the pavements outside their homes. Most of the city schools had reopened by the end of May.

At first, civilians were allowed to queue up at the Red Army soup kitchens throughout the city, then on 15 May the defunct Nazi ration cards were replaced by a new system that reflected Soviet values and the practical demands of rebuilding a crushed city. Manual workers and the rubble-women received considerably more calories than the elderly, who were unable to contribute a great deal to the necessary work in hand. Their ration cards were quickly nicknamed 'the cemetery ticket'.

Crime, disease and death

Despite Barzarin's best efforts, before his untimely death in June, life in Berlin was harsh throughout Year Zero. The city was home to an army of homeless, destitute and war-damaged Berliners who had lost everything, and often everybody, in their lives. Inevitably crime was rampant with unprecedented levels of murder, robbery and rape among the civilian population. Elements of the Red Army also still posed a threat to civilians, especially when they had been drinking.

The meagre, dull rations encouraged a thriving black market where the currencies needed to buy a little extra food were cigarettes, jewellery, watches and sex. Throughout that first summer of Allied occupation, most Berliners were underweight and hungry and diseases like diphtheria took their toll in the unusually warm weather.

Following that, many were ill-prepared for the '*Elendswinter*', the miserably cruel winter of 1945–46 that was the coldest for many years. Over a thousand Berliners died from hypothermia and the death toll was only kept under control by the provision of public heated rooms, where the population could shelter from temperatures that dipped as low as minus 25 degrees.

Prisoners of war

The effort to rebuild the city was not helped by the lack of fit young manpower. By the end of the war approximately 3 million German soldiers were prisoners of war in Russian hands. The Soviets claimed to hold 2.8 million Germans captive, but West German analysts later estimated that the figure had been nearer 3.1 million.

Of these, the Russians maintained that around 385,000 had died in captivity. The West German figure was significantly higher, however: it was thought that somewhere

The burnt-out shell of the Adlon Hotel on Unter den Linden stands next to a giant poster of Stalin erected by the Russians.

between 700,000 and 1.1 million prisoners had lost their lives in Russia. Most of these prisoners did some time as manual labourers, undertaking elementary reconstruction work in Russian cities. There was, therefore, a significant labour shortage in eastern Germany until the early 1950s, when many of these POWs began to be released.

There remained behind in the USSR approximately 85,000 to 90,000 German prisoners, who had been convicted of war crimes. Most of the bunker inhabitants fell into this category, if only because their proximity to Hitler implied that they must have been avid supporters of Nazism.

Many had been given prison terms of up to 25 years. As the last of these POWs were marched east into an uncertain future, another wave of desperate people was fleeing in the opposite direction, towards Germany and Austria: the ethnic Germans of central and eastern Europe.

Fate of the ethnic Germans

There had always been significant numbers of ethnic Germans living in the patchwork of states and identities of central and eastern Europe. Some had supported Hitlerism and had occupied positions within the Nazi regimes that invaded and absorbed Czechoslovakia, Poland and Yugoslavia after 1938. Others had been happy to live in the democratic nations created by the Versailles Settlement and had played no significant part in the occupation and exploitation of these lands under the Nazis. In 1945, however, all were identified with the brutal identity politics of the Nazi regimes that had briefly ruled over these territories, simply by being German.

Continuing German atrocities

There had always been tensions between Germans and Slavs throughout central and eastern Europe. Now this old antipathy had been sharpened by the ideological struggle between Nazism and Communism and by the scale of atrocities carried out by German agencies during the Third Reich. Even when the war was clearly lost, SS units in these territories continued to carry out acts of extreme brutality towards local populations. Prisoners in Nazi camps were executed at a frenzied pace and civilians were rounded up and shot on the slightest suspicion of being potentially hostile.

Dozens of anecdotes tell of group round-ups and mass shootings that served no point whatsoever, other than to stoke up the desire for revenge. As the Red Army approached and liberated territories under Nazi control, the German authorities were initially reluctant to consider organizing an official evacuation of German communities. Evacuation was too easily mistaken back in Berlin for defeatism, for which the penalties were severe. As a result, millions of German speakers were left stranded in states where they were no longer welcome.

Slav reprisals

Slav leaders in Poland, Czechoslovakia, Yugoslavia, Romania and Hungary all saw an opportunity for a final solution to the German problem in their territories. Thousands of Germans were now about to learn what it had been like to be a Jew, a Gypsy or even just a Slav in Nazi-occupied Europe. The humiliations and punishments that ethnic Germans, and suspected collaborators, suffered in the last days of the war were designed to imitate those meted out by the Germans before the fortunes of war changed.

In many Czech and Polish towns, Germans were required to wear a white armband bearing a large black letter N, for Nemetz, the Slavic core word for German. This made them easy targets in the street for any expression of rage and disgust. There were numerous cases of Germans being taken by angry mobs and drowned in fast-flowing rivers.

German houses, farms and businesses were forfeited and given to new Slavic residents.

If Germans were allowed to stay in a settlement, they were herded into a ghetto of damaged buildings or sheds. Many ethnic Germans found themselves interned in former Nazi concentration camps, where they were treated little better than Jews, socialists and other enemies of the Reich had fared. Seven hundred Germans were interned at the Hanke camp in Ostrava in northern Czechoslovakia. Of these, 231 died, mostly as a result of horrific injuries from torture, beatings, gang rape and random killings. Germans were also hunted down in public buildings such as churches and hospitals and casually executed.

Expulsions

Women who had collaborated with German troops or officials received the usual public humiliation of being stripped and beaten in public and their hair shorn or tarred. And men and women who had in happier times contracted marriages across the nationality divide were also arrested and punished. Rounded up by the Czech police, thousands of Germans were marched at gunpoint to the Austrian border. Just as the Jews had found a few weeks before, when forced to endure death marches westwards, there was little humanity shown to the frail, the elderly or the young who failed to keep up. On 12 May, the new president of Czechoslovakia, Edvard Beneš, voiced the anger and lust for revenge that was felt by Slavs across liberated eastern Europe: 'The German people behaved like a monster. We must end the German problem once and for all.'

Approximately 30,000 Germans died during the first phase of expulsions from Czechoslovakia and the figure was far higher in the lands that had been German but were now in Polish hands.

In all, between 1944 and 1946 more than 14 million ethnic Germans disappeared from lands that they had inhabited for hundreds of years.

From the very earliest days of his political career, Hitler had dreamed of creating a vast Germanic empire stretching to the Urals. In his vision of the future, the existing ethnic German populations of central and eastern Europe would be joined by millions of new Aryan colonists. Instead, by the end of 1946 the old Germans of the East had simply ceased to exist.

Epilogue
Misinformation and Myths

All of the confusion about Hitler's fate began before the Russians had completed their conquest of Berlin. The German version, that Hitler and Eva Braun had taken their own lives and had been cremated, was relayed to Stalin by Marshal Zhukov before dawn on 1 May. Initially, Stalin seemed to have accepted this account and expressed his regret that it had not been possible to capture 'the bastard' alive. Moscow announced the deaths of Hitler and Goebbels by their own hands via a radio communiqué broadcast on the evening of 2 May and several statements issued by Russian sources in Berlin during the coming weeks of May and June 1945 generally confirmed that Hitler was dead.

The Supreme Allied Commanders, meeting in the city in early June, were then informed that his body had been discovered and identified with 'almost complete certainty'. An officer from Zhukov's staff also informed Allied journalists that the charred remains of Hitler and his wife had been uncovered. Despite the damage inflicted by Soviet flamethrowers during what the Russians called 'the storming of the Führerbunker', it was claimed that enough of the two corpses remained to permit a thorough scientific examination and a certain identification.

However, in more private discussions with American and other Allied representatives, Stalin had begun to express his opinion that 'the bastard' was not in fact dead but had escaped from Berlin and was now in hiding in some prearranged bolt-hole with Goebbels and Bormann.

Hitler's death doubted

During the summer of 1945, Stalin's personal opinion gradually became the official Soviet line. Marshal Zhukov, who had been quite sure in early May that Hitler was dead, was by 9 June stating in public that Hitler might well be alive. Now it seemed that the Soviets had not found a corpse that could be positively identified as Hitler. The Führer's whereabouts were, in fact, a mystery and it was quite possible that he had been flown from Berlin to a place of refuge, with other members of the Nazi elite. When he was asked where he thought Hitler might be, Zhukov had replied that it was 'up to the British and Americans to find him'.

Stalin was certainly coming around to the view that Hitler's old friend, the Fascist dictator General Franco, was involved in this increasingly murky escapade. In the last days of April, German radio had placed a great deal of emphasis upon the fact that Hitler was in the capital city masterminding every detail of its defence and Goebbels had imagined that such a message would inspire the beleaguered citizenry. Stalin increasingly suspected that this emphasis upon Hitler remaining at the helm of state was a smokescreen to mask the fact that he was already somewhere else.

The Soviets and the other Allies already knew about the flurry of planes that left Berlin for Munich on 22 and 23 April. According to the story emerging from the interrogation of the captured bunkerites, the passengers on those last flights were old friends and retainers of the Führer, such as his secretary Johanna Wolf and his physician Dr Morell. That seemed unlikely to Stalin. He reckoned that the despicable Hitler would have prioritized saving his own skin before that of his subordinates.

Then there was the fact that both of Hitler's pilots, Hans Baur and Georg Betz, were known to have been in the government quarter close to the bunker throughout the last days of the regime.

Their presence had worried Hitler when he feared that he might be whisked away to Bavaria against his will and now it was worrying Stalin. There was also some information about several planes escaping from Berlin late on 30 April in the direction of Hamburg and rumours of a submarine waiting in the Baltic. Later in the summer, a Nazi submarine was said to have arrived at Mar del Plata on the coast of Argentina.

Stalin's suspicions were easily aroused, for he had always felt uncomfortable about the Soviet Union's alliance of convenience with the capitalist Western states. He could imagine changed circumstances in the future where the old Führer might prove to be a useful tool for the British and the Americans. Stalin could still not get it out of his mind that somehow Franco was involved. He had made several speeches in 1945 and 1946 castigating the Western democracies for allowing an openly Fascist state to continue to survive in their midst.

Idea of suicide rejected

And the very idea of Hitler calmly sitting down on his sofa and serenely raising a pistol to his head didn't sit well with Stalin's understanding of his arch-enemy. Stalin knew that Hitler was smart and cunning and an old street-fighter. He could not believe that he had just given up and stayed in Berlin to possibly face the inevitable show trial and an inglorious death at the end of a Russian rope.

Stalin compared Hitler's supposed actions with his own in 1941 when he also found himself in a tight spot. The Wehrmacht had smashed its way through western Russia and was at the very edge of Moscow. It seemed unstoppable at that point, while the Soviet forces had been routed and were dispirited.

Stalin's desperate reaction in the face of almost certain defeat was not to go down with the Soviet ship of state, but to flee and live to fight another day. Throughout the tense battle for Moscow, a specially equipped and armoured locomotive stood waiting underneath the Kremlin to carry him as far east as possible into the heartland of the Soviet Union, a mode of transport partly dictated by his fear of flying and by the fact that the Luftwaffe temporarily controlled the Russian skies. Stalin had been prepared to flee and abandon his capital and he assumed that his arch-enemy would be ready to do the same.

Nowhere to hide

Stalin was very aware that Hitler was not stupid. Like him, he must have made his preparations in case of defeat, he thought. He had to be hiding in the Alps or in Fascist Spain or in some other friendly state where the CIA could shelter him until needed. There was no shortage of Hitler 'sightings' after the war. In fact, throughout the late 1940s and early 1950s Hitler was supposedly spotted on a global tour that took in Spain, Portugal, Brazil, Japan and Tibet. He could, of course, afford to travel in some style because it seemed vast treasures had also been spirited out of the Reich on that last plane from Berlin.

But Stalin failed to take account of the fact that Hitler had no vast hinterland in which to escape. The so-called Alpine Redoubt in Bavaria would have been an inconvenience for the advancing Americans but would only have delayed Hitler's capture by a matter of days. Then would come the ignominy of the humiliating photographs of a handcuffed, beaten loser being dragged into court and then accompanied to the scaffold.

Moreover, like most Germans, Stalin had seen few images of Hitler since Stalingrad. He had little conception of how much Hitler had aged and wearied in recent years and become tired of the war. He could not imagine that his great and deadly foe was now reduced to a shambling, trembling wreck. Stalin would not have believed that the great warlord had almost lost all interest in the war that he had inflicted upon the world.

Bunkerites fail to agree facts

The interrogation evidence from the captured bunkerites also confirmed Stalin's suspicion that Hitler's disappearance may have been planned well before the end of hostilities. The testimonies emerging from Linge, Kempka, Günsche and all the others were ambiguous and contradictory at almost every point in the story. There was confusion about every main detail. Was it believable that these associates, living together in that compressed underground atmosphere, could not agree on so many details of the important events that unfolded, and that they witnessed at close quarters, on 29 and 30 April?

The bunkerites were bombarded with a torrent of questions. At what time was the Hitler wedding held? Did Hitler dictate his last will and testament before or after the wedding? When had Hitler and Eva killed themselves? How had they killed themselves? Did anyone really hear the shot that Hitler was supposed to have fired? In particular, why was there so much confusion about that vital point in the tale?

The survivors who entered Hitler's study and apparently first saw the dead bodies could not even agree on the scene they witnessed. Was Eva Braun sitting or lying across the sofa? Who carried the bodies up to the garden? Which body was carried up first? Where exactly in the garden had the bodies been cremated? How thoroughly were the bodies burned? Was there sufficient petrol to do the job properly? How long did they burn for? Crucially, why did Hitler's closest staff, who had been entrusted to ensure that the body of their beloved Führer was completely annihilated, not bother to go back up the steps to check? Was it because they knew he wasn't really there?

The answers to these questions, which Stalin's interrogators were now harvesting from the captive bunkerites, often differed considerably. Was it really possible that these loyal supporters of the Führer could disagree so much about what was evidently one of the most significant moments in their lives and in world history? Were the differences in their testimonies really just the result of the tension of the moment? Or were they carefully planned?

Why the testimonies varied

It all seemed part of a put-up job to the canny dictator in the Kremlin. Stalin was convinced that the sharply conflicting testimonies were designed to complicate any investigation and to baffle the inquisitors. And even if this was not the case, if 'the bastard' really had been burned to ash, the idea of a conspiracy to save and protect Hitler might turn out to be useful in his future dealings with the Western states, who were rapidly becoming his 'former' allies.

Stalin failed to appreciate the oppressive atmosphere of fear and tension that had dominated the lives of the bunker inhabitants in the last weeks of the war. He continually asked why it was that these people did not accurately remember such immense events, failing to appreciate that they were unable to recall them accurately precisely because they *were* so immense and because they mattered so much to the participants.

Many of the witnesses had lived most of their adult lives alongside Hitler. They were in awe of him at times and to some degree in fear of him, but the dictator had been a big part of their existence.

When the Führer took his own life, it was a traumatic experience for them, not least because a shadow of fear and uncertainty about their own lives then hung over them all. Added to that, some of the bunkerites were unwell before they were captured and the conditions they experienced in Soviet captivity did nothing to improve their health. It was also clear that the quantities of alcohol consumed on 29 and 30 April had obscured the memory and judgement of several of the key participants.

The answers that they gave to Soviet interrogators were, of course, given under duress, after threats and in some cases during and after beatings and torture. There was inevitably an element of shaping responses to meet the expected requirements of the interrogator but also to protect their own futures. While in Soviet captivity, they fearfully tended to minimize their own personal importance in the saga of Hitler's death.

Stories changed over time

Once released and free in West Germany to write their memoirs, they inevitably emphasized and exaggerated their contribution to this dramatic moment in history. Others, like Kempka the chauffeur, changed their stories over time as their memories were challenged and refined by the publications of others.

Some witnesses in the bunker group, like Traudl Junge, changed their testimony as a result of simply maturing, and of thinking more deeply about the events of 1939 to 1945. Her earlier view of her time in the bunker was much influenced by her personal relationships with the key personalities. Her later comments were guided more by her reflection upon the awful consequences of National Socialist values and policies upon Germany and the wider world.

Search for physical evidence

None of this satisfied Stalin. The garden behind the Reich Chancellery continued to be examined for weeks on end in the extensive search for more evidence. Every single particle in the garden was sifted through two wire meshes of differing fineness.

Many bits and pieces of bone were salvaged and two of these were of particular interest. One was a lower jawbone with some teeth and some evidence of two dental bridges.

The other was part of an upper jaw with a gold dental bridge and several porcelain facets. From these exhibits and their surroundings, a total of 15 teeth were collected.

Fortunately, the Soviets had Hitler's personal dentist Hugo Blaschke in their custody, along with Blaschke's dental technician and dental assistant. Understandably, all three had taken a great interest and pride in the treatment they had given the Führer. They remembered the exact specifications of the work they had done for him and could correctly identify the fragments. A piece of cranial bone later recovered from the garden also seemed to be associated with the dental remains.

Had Hitler used a double?

Stalin was still not convinced. For a while he was intrigued by the idea that Hitler had employed a double in his escape plans. Was it actually Hitler's double who was shot and cremated on 30 April while the real Führer took the plane that left Tiergarten that evening for Hamburg and the waiting submarine bound for South America? In his later memoir, Linge touched on this idea, arguing that the Führer would have been embarrassed to use a double. Hitler was proud of the fact that he could appear among his people without fear, although he hadn't done so very often since the war began to turn badly against Germany.

Nevertheless, there were rumours of a remarkably close double, identified by the SS in 1941 and secretly kept sedated and under arrest in case he was ever needed. Stalin continued to be intrigued and irritated by these rumours and questions surrounding Hitler's demise, right up until his own death in 1953.

Enduring fascination with Hitler

He was not alone. A morbid interest in all the minutiae relating to the history, imagery and mythology of the Nazi Age has not abated while public interest in his contemporary, Stalin, has faded over time. Stalin was a dictator who rivalled Hitler in many ways. Like Hitler, he was a mass murderer who probably liquidated just as many human beings, if not more, than his Austro-German rival. His casual attitude to the destruction of millions of inconvenient people who had no place in his plans for a future world was little different from Hitler's. Yet there is comparatively little public interest in Stalin outwith academic historical circles.

Perhaps this is because Stalin's murderous persecutions were essentially domestic affairs, conducted in distant, little-known parts of the Soviet Union and often carried out in pursuit of mundane economic policies such as the collectivization of agrarian production. Stalin's ultimate aim was to preside over an industrialized economy run to some degree on the principles of a totalitarian Marxist–Leninist state. A dreary beehive. His evil works were largely done in secret and few images remain. Their horror has had to be dug out from obscure party documents deep in the Russian archives.

By contrast, Hitler's rise, decline and fall was a narrative about one unusual personality, and a drama conducted on a much more public, international stage. Hitler's ultimate goal was nothing less than world domination and the reshaping of the human population.

From the outset, Hitler had understood the power of imagery in spreading his ideas and values, and in masking their flaws and consequences. Every Nazi event was choreographed. Every photographic and cinematographic trick was used to embellish the Nazi vision, to illustrate and exaggerate the power of the movement and the perceived inevitability of its triumph.

Everything filmed or photographed

Apart from the bloody beatings of dissenters in German back alleyways in the early days or the sudden and unexpected murder of Hitler's critics in the SA in 1934, no episode in the Nazi saga was left unfilmed or unphotographed. The Nazi Party was proud to film and broadcast its most brutal moments. Nazi newsreels not only featured the destruction of Jewish property and the public humiliation and degradation of Jewish victims, but they also glorified it. Even the most horrific crimes in the death camps of the Holocaust were filmed by the SS for the educational benefit of posterity. Almost every chapter in the history of Hitler and his murderous regime is known to us through the vast photographic and film archive that survived his bloody end – apart from the last few deadly moments. There were no cameras in the Führerbunker.

Hidden last moments

We cannot see into the last act of the Hitler drama, those final days in the bunker. We are left only with the confused and conflicting memories of the very few survivors beneath the Citadel of Berlin, and they were entirely overwhelmed by emotion, tension, exhaustion and fear. The last moments in Hitler's life continue to appal and fascinate in equal measure because we cannot watch them. They were acted out in deep secrecy.

We have to imagine for ourselves the bloody conclusion of the fundamental enigma that was Adolf Hitler and we can only wonder about the final moment in his downfall and destruction as he slowly raised the pistol to his head.

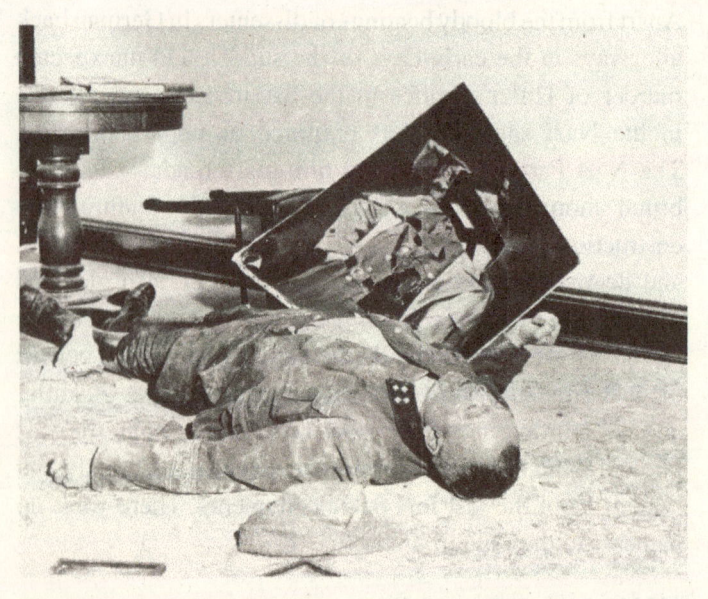

The body of a Volkssturm *general lies on the floor of City Hall with a torn picture of the Führer next to it. Adolf Hitler promised to make Germany great again, but his legacy was defeat, devastation and decades of division.*

Further Reading: Eyewitness Accounts

With Hitler to the End
The memoirs of Hitler's valet, Heinz Linge, 2009

I Was Hitler's Chauffeur
The memoirs of Erich Kempka, 1951

Until the Final Hour
Memoirs of Hitler's last secretary, Traudl Junge, 2004

He Was My Chief
The memoirs of Adolf Hitler's secretary, Christa Schroeder, 1985

In the Bunker with Hitler
The last witness speaks, Bernd Freytag von Loringhoven, 2006

In Hitler's Bunker
A boy soldier's eyewitness account of the Führer's last days, Armin D Lehmann, 2004

The Last Witness
The memoirs of Hitler's bodyguard, Rochus Misch, 2014

Mini-glossary

Aryan
used by Nazis to describe pure Germanic peoples

Führerstadt
honorary title given to Linz, Hitler's boyhood town

Hofbrauhaus
Munich beerhall where Hitler gave his first speeches

NKVD
Soviet secret police during the World War II period

Putsch
an armed uprising to take over the government

Sturmabteilung/Storm Department
a Nazi paramilitary organization

Tiergarten
a large park with zoo in central Berlin

Völkisch
an ethnic nationalist view of German culture and politics

Waffen SS
military wing of the SS that fought alongside the regular German army or Wehrmacht

Index

Aachen, Battle of 82–3
Adenauer, Konrad 163
Alfieri, Dino 51
Alpine Redoubt 133, 179
Ardennes Offensive 14, 113–14
Axmann, Artur 131, 133, 161, 162
Baarová, Lìda 156
Baur, Hans 23, 63, 163, 166, 177
Bechstein, Helene 46–7
Below, Nicolaus von 77
Beneš, Edvard 173
Berghof, the 19, 54, 55, 58
Bernadotte, Count 33
Berlin
    Hitler's dreams for 9
    siege of 15–16, 92–3
    life in during siege 75–80
    start of siege 86–8
    atrocities in 93
    rape in 95–9, 101–3
    Russian acts of kindness in 103–4
    battle for Reichstag 107–11
    Volkssturm in 121
    Felix Steiner's defence of 127–8
    surrender of 166–7
    order restored in 167–8
    harshness of life in 169
Berzarin, Nikolai 167, 168, 169
Betz, Georg 23, 63, 162, 177
Blaschke, Hugo 183
Blondi 138, 139
Bormann, Martin 25
    career under Hitler 18–20
    and Paula Hitler 21
    in Hitler's Political Testament 25
    in Hitler's Last Will 22, 26
    and Hermann Göring 29, 31
    at marriage of Eva Braun and Hitler 39
    confirms Aryan purity of Eva Braun 53
    life in the bunker 74
    at Hitler's suicide 130–1, 133, 145, 146–7
    attempts ceasefire 158
    death of 162
Brandt, Karl 54, 66, 71
Braun, Eva
    last day of 7, 8
    and Paula Hitler 21
    and Hermann Fegelein 35
    marriage to Hitler announced 35–6
    wedding ceremony 37–40, 59
    first meets Hitler 40, 53
    relationship with Hitler 53–9
    life in the bunker 74
    plans suicide 85–6, 137
    suicide of 129, 131, 132, 140–2
    courage of 144
    disposal of corpse 144–7, 149, 175–6
Braun, Franziska 'Fanny' 22
Braun, Gretl 54
Breslau 117
Bulge, Battle of the 14
Burgdorf, General 74, 131, 147, 160
Chamberlain, Houston Stewart 49
Chamberlain, Neville 56
Christian, Gerda 85–6, 141, 163
Chuikov, General 158–9
Churchill, Winston 24, 123, 125
Ciano, Galeazzo 50
Czechoslovakia 171, 172–4
Darré, Richard Walter 31–2
Deedes, Bill 101
Demmin 104
Dönitz, Admiral 126
    command of army in Baltic 15
    in Hitler's Political Testament 26
    and battle for Reichstag 107
Eastern Front

190 INDEX

German losses on 111–13, 115
Eckart, Dietrich 51–2
Ehrenburg, Ilya 102, 133
Eichmann, Adolf 19
Einsatzgruppen 32
Eisenhower, General 102
Elizabeth, Princess 124
ethnic Germans 171, 172–4
Fegelein, Hermann 34–5
Fortress Cities 116–17
Franco, General 176, 177
Frederick the Great 124, 130
Freiburg 99
Fuchsl 138
Führerstadt (Linz) 18–19
Germany
    war-weariness in 80
    disintegration of Nazi Party in 80, 81–3
    Russian surprise at prosperity in 93–5
    rape by occupying powers 99–101
Giesing, Erwin 57, 70–1
Giesler, Hermann 17
Goebbels, Helga 151, 153
Goebbels, Helmuth 130
Goebbels, Joseph 57
    and Hitler's Last Will and Political Testament 14, 25
    at marriage of Eva Braun and Hitler 39
    tours bombed cities 71
    and food supplies for Berlin 75
    and German war-weariness 80, 83
    and Hitler's last radio broadcast 82
    and Nemmersdorf massacre 89, 90
    and Ferdinand Schörner 126
    and Hitler's suicide 133, 142, 147
    kills own children 151–3
    suicide of 154
    loyalty to Hitler 154–6
    life in bunker 158–60
    attempts ceasefire 158–9
Goebbels, Magda 55, 57, 129, 142, 151–4, 154, 156, 158
Göring, Emmy 55
Göring, Hermann
    career under Hitler 27–9
    sends telegram to Hitler 29, 31
    leaves Berlin 154
    Hitler's view of 155–6
Greim, Robert Ritter von 26–7
Günsche, Otto 124, 130–1, 135–6, 141, 145–6, 163, 179
Haase, Werner 61–2, 140, 164
Hanke, Karl 156
Hasselbach, Hanskarl von 70, 71
Hauschild, Fritz 65
Hentschel, Johannes 164
Hess, Rudolf 18, 19, 41, 49
Hewel, Walther 160
Heydrich, Reinhard 32–3
Himmler, Heinrich
    command of Waffen SS in Baltic 15
    career under Hitler 31–3
    offer of surrender to Allies 33–4, 137
    and German war-weariness 83
    and Hitler's suicide plans 89, 137
    becomes army commander 120–2
    and Felix Steiner 127
    leaves Berlin 154
    Hitler's view of 155–6
Hitler, Adolf
    last day of 7
    reminiscing about past 7–8, 123–4
    sense of remorse 9–10
    as sociopath 10–13
    dictates Last Will and Political Testament 13–14
    enters Berlin bunker 14–16
    contents of Last Will 16–24
    and Martin Bormann 18, 19, 20
    family members 20–2
    contents of Political Testament 24–7, 31, 34, 126
    and Hermann Göring 27–8, 29, 155–6
    and Heinrich Himmler 31, 33–4, 155–6
    and Hermann Fegelein 34–5
    announces marriage to Eva Braun 35–6
    wedding ceremony 37–40, 59
    first meets Eva Braun 40

sexuality of 41–4
relationships with women 44–52
relationship with Eva Braun 53–9
deteriorating health of 61–5, 67–72
last public appearance 72–3
final radio broadcast 82
plans suicide 85–6, 89, 132–40
and battle for Reichstag 111
intransigence over Stalingrad 112
and Ardennes Offensive 113, 114
military knowledge of 114, 115–16
makes Himmler army commander 120–2
disillusionment with war 122–5
concedes war is lost 128
suicide of 129–40
courage of 142–4
disposal of corpse 144–7, 149, 175
death of announced 147–8, 175–6
and Joseph Goebbels 155–6
doubts over death 176–83
fascination with 184–5
Hitler, Angela 21, 54
Hitler, Heinz 22
Hitler, Klara 20–1, 130
Hitler, Paula 21, 46
Hitler, William Henry 22
Hofbeck, Hans 146
Hoffmann, Frau 54
Hoffmann, Heinrich 73
Holocaust, the
  and Martin Bormann 19
Höss, Rudolf 18
Hotel Adlon 101
Irwin, Virginia 79, 106
Junge, Gertraud 'Traudl'
  dictation of Hitler's Last Will and Political Testament 13, 14
  and marriage of Hitler and Eva Braun 36
  and suicide of Eva Braun and Hitler 85–6, 132, 141–2
  and Goebbels children 152
  arrest and release 161
  later reflections of 182
Karstadt department store 87–8

Kempa, Erich 23, 72, 73, 76, 79, 136, 137, 146–7, 165, 179, 182
Kersten, Felix 122
Konev, General 102
Königsberg 91–2, 117
Krasnaya Zvezda (Red Star) 102
Krebs, General 74, 131, 147, 158–9, 160
Kroll Opera House 108, 111
Kronika, Jacob 75
Krüger, Else 161–2
Kubizek, August 43, 134
Kunz, Helmut 151
Kursk, Battle of 113
Laffert, Baroness Sigrid von 'Sigi' 8, 50–1, 53
Lake Constance 99
Lasch, Otto 91
Last Will of Adolf Hitler 13–14, 16–24
Lehmann, Armin 68–9, 76
Lehndorf, Hans von 91
Leignitz 95
Ley, Robert 135
Lindloff, Ewald 149
Linge, Frau 59
Linge, Heinz 56, 61, 67, 74, 124, 129, 130–1, 135–66, 140, 142, 145, 146, 147, 165–6, 179, 183
Linz 17–18
Manziarly, Constanze 141, 148, 162–3
Maurice, Emil 41–2, 130
Mein Kampf (Hitler) 49, 54
Messerschmitt ME 163 Komet 117–18
Misch, Rochus 152–3, 164
Mittlstrasser, Gretel 56
Mohnke, Wilhelm 141, 160, 164
Molotov, Vyacheslav 125
Morell, Theodor 62–5, 70–1, 89, 137, 177
Müller, Renate 42, 45
Mussolini, Benito 14, 69, 139
Naumann, Werner 161
Nazi Party
  disintegration of 80, 81–3
Negus 138–9
Nemmersdorf massacre 89–90

Neustadt am Rübenberge 100
Night of the Long Knives 44
O'Brien, Toby 57
Oppenhoff, Franz 83
Ostertag, Liesl 141
Pervitin 65–6
Petacci, Clara 139
Peter III, Emperor 124
Poland 171, 172
Political Testament of Adolf Hitler 13–14, 24–7, 31, 34, 126
Potsdam 125
prisoners of war 169–71
Quandt, Günther 159
Quandt, Harald 159–60
Raubal, Angela 'Geli' 42, 44–5, 53
Raubal, Leo 21
Rauschning, Hermann 41, 43
Rehborn, Anni 54
Reich Chancellery
    stormed by Russians 15
    Eva Braun's room in 55
    looted by Russian soldiers 101
Reichstag
    battle for 107–11, 140
Reinhardt, Generaloberst 90
Reisser, Hans 149
Reiter, Maria 'Mitzi' 45–6, 52
Reitsch, Hanna 26
Riefenstahl, Leni 8, 51
Rienzi (Wagner) 134
Rienzo, Cola di 134–5
Röhm, Ernst 41, 44
Rommell, Erwin 65
Roosevelt, Franklin D. 124
Schaub, Julius 23
Schenck, Ernst 164
Schörner, Ferdinand 26, 125–6
Schreck, Julius 23
Schwägermann, Günter 154
Schwerer Gustav railway cannon 118
Schwielow Lake 125
Seelow Heights 86, 87, 92, 127
Seyss-Inquart, Arthur 26

Shatilov, Vasily 109
Soviet Union
    German losses on 111–13, 115
Speer, Albert 133, 154
Speer, Margarete 54
Stalin, Joseph
    and treatment of German civilians 102, 105–6
    and battle for Reichstag 109, 111
    disagreements with Churchill 125
    obsession over Hitler's death 139, 159, 175, 176, 177–9, 181, 182
    as historic figure 184
Stalin, Yakov 21
Stalingrad, Battle of 111–12
Stasi 138–9
Steiner, Felix 127–8
Strasser, Gregor 44–5
Strasser, Otto 44
Stumpfegger, Ludwig 132, 137, 147, 151–2, 162
Tornow, Fritz 138
Truman, Harry 125
U-boats 118–19
V1 and V2 rockets 118
Volkssturm 120–1
Wagner, Richard 47, 67, 134
Wagner, Siegfried 47–8
Wagner, Walter 37, 39, 59
Wagner, Winifred 47–50
Weidling, General 68, 140, 141, 166–7
Wenck, General 73, 125
Wessel, Horst 51
Wiedemann, Fritz 51
Winter, Frau 22
Wolf, Johanna 23, 177
Wollenhaupt, August 58, 68
wonder weapons 117–18
Zhukov, General 102, 127–8, 159, 176